D0876044

United in Beauty:
The Jewelry and Collectors of
Linda MacNeil

[signature]

2009

Schiffer Publishing Ltd

4880 Lower Valley Road, Atglen, PA 19310 USA

cover
Lotus Necklace, 1999
acid polished clear Waterford Crystal,
polished green glass detail, 14k yellow gold
6 1/2 inches diam.
Collection Mint Museum of Craft and Design,
donated by Waterford Crystal Ltd. & Linda MacNeil
in honor of Chris Rifkin
Photo: ©Bill Truslow

above
Babylon Fragment Brooch, 2002
acid polished amber glass, polished 14k yellow gold
2 x 2 x 1/2 inches
with earrings

Contents

Library of Congress Cataloging-in-Publication Data

MacNeil, Linda, 1954-
    United in Beauty : the jewelry and collectors of Linda MacNeil / by Linda MacNeil
    ISBN 0-7643-1712-1
    p. cm.
1. MacNeil, Linda, 1954—Catalogs. 2. Jewelry—United States—History—20th century—Catalogs. I. Title: Jewelry and collectors of Linda MacNeil. II. Title.
    NK7398.M33 A4 2002
    739.27'092—dc21
                    2002006633

Copyright © 2000 & 2002 by Schiffer Publishing, Ltd.
All rights reserved. No part of this work may be reproduced or used in any form or by any means—graphic, electronic, or mechanical, including photocopying or information storage and retrieval systems—without written permission from the copyright holder.

Book Design by: Joe Rapone
Typeset in Garamond and Univers
ISBN: 0-7643-1712-1
Printed in China
1 2 3 4

Published by Schiffer Publishing Ltd.
4880 Lower Valley Road
Atglen, PA 19310
Phone: (610) 593-1777; Fax: (610) 593-2002
E-mail: Schifferbk@aol.com
Please visit our web site catalog at
www.schifferbooks.com

This book may be purchased from the publisher.
Include $3.95 for shipping. Please try your bookstore first.
We are always looking for people to write books on new and related subjects. If you have an idea for a book please contact us at the above address.
You may write for a free catalog.

In Europe, Schiffer books are distributed by
Bushwood Books
6 Marksbury Avenue
Kew Gardens
Surrey TW9 4JF England
Phone: 44 (0) 20-8392-8585; Fax: 44 (0) 20-8392-9876
E-mail: Bushwd@aol.com
Free postage in the UK. Europe: air mail at cost.

©2002 Suzanne Ramljak, "United in Beauty: The Jewelry and Collectors of Linda MacNeil"
© 2002 Helen W. Drutt English, "Linda's Web"
© Portrait Photography: John Carlano
Portrait Makeup: Angella Mendillo
Photography of works:
© Susie Cushner, pages 13, 16–22, 32, 34, 36, 38, 41, 46, 48, 70, 72, 81
© Charles Mayer, pages 50, 51, 55, 59
© Bill Truslow, pages 2, 3, 23, 24, 25, 35, 56, 60– 68, 74–79, 85–199
Dimensions are given in inches; height precedes depth, precedes width.

Linda MacNeil

Dedicated to Dan Dailey

At first, I thought about having professional models wearing my jewelry for this book. However, I realized that this was an opportunity to celebrate the women who have collected these pieces and therefore supported my art over the years. When I asked them to sit for portraits, their response was overwhelmingly positive.

I owe thanks to all of the women for taking the time and traveling to one of seven photo sessions we had in various locations around the United States. Because of their participation, the relationship between the jewelry and the wearer is honestly shown, and the sense of adornment that I pursue in each piece is illustrated with a great variety of personalities. My sincere thanks to the sponsors who supported my idea of a book showing collectors; they have my highest respect and heartfelt gratitude.

I also thank the photographers, makeup artist and designer who traveled to all of the portrait locations and worked long hours to get the best possible results. Due to the dedicated efforts of everyone involved who made this project possible, my dream has become a reality.

–LM

Linda's Web

by
Helen W. Drutt English

A drawer is opened to reveal a necklace within a velvet case. There is a quality of richness that engages the eyes, forcing one to look at its form while marveling at its elegance. It is there, waiting for someone to lift it out of that solitary space where it has been hidden and protected from view. A hand reaches in and eyes contemplate its beauty while thinking about the artist who conceived it. It has another life as it is draped like a flexible bridge between two hands. The necklace hangs gracefully suspended in the air. It is being lifted then placed around the neck of the owner. Another episode in its journey into the public forum begins.

How is that work transformed? Does it change with every individual? What happens to the necklace as it meets its destined owner? Is there a connection between the wearer and the work that gives it a new identity? The necklaces and portraits in this book are all woven together by the common threads of the artist and in this case, the photographer, John Carlano. Here is an opportunity to contemplate Linda MacNeil's works and their visual transformation as they are worn by her community of patrons. There is a visual comfort in these portraits, which connect with each other to spin Linda's golden and crystal web—like the threads of a tapestry weaving a history of her creative works.

Eighty portraits documenting Linda's collectors, who are largely drawn from the contemporary craft movement, invite us to experience her work while being worn. The necklaces have journeyed to locations throughout the United States. In a recent review of the "Virtue and Beauty" exhibition at the National Gallery of Art in Washington, D.C., critic Robert Hughes stated that portraiture as we know it is the "art of making recognizable likeness of individuals."[1] This art, coupled with MacNeil's desire to document her jewelry and its relationship to the patron, is yet another history in itself.

Photographic portraits in the twentieth century frequently depicted the subjects as foils for their possessions. Think of Man Ray's portrait of Nancy Cunard; her image becomes a background for a collection of African ivory bracelets, her eyes are cast away from the camera and her dream-like appearance enhances her possessions. Likewise, his portrait of Jacqueline is "a living model turned to stone to present inanimate jewelry."[2] In the 1983 portrait of Louisa Calder, her face is not revealed but her gesture clearly exhibits Alexander's coiled ring and hairpiece as compared with Georgia O'Keefe's striking portrait in which we must "discover" her OK brooch by Calder.[3]

How do we count the ways in which we celebrate ornaments and their patrons? The 1987 catalogue that documented "Europea Joieria Contem-porania," in Barcelona, was revolutionary. Outstanding figures of the social and artistic life of Spain served as models for the jewelry. Their gestures and persona dramatically altered the documentation of the various ornaments, influencing one's response to them. The catalogue spearheaded a change in the history of jewelry documen-tation. In 1994, Giampaolo Babetto's *Ritratti* was published. The artist's retrospective was presented through photographic portraits of the owners wearing his work; color photographs subdued the individuals, bringing the works to the forefront of the photograph. Breon O'Casey's 70th Birthday was heralded with surprise photo booklets of his patrons adorned with his work. From far and near they came to Philadelphia to be photographed; the individuals who are the collectors form another connection to the artist and become a distinct and recognizable community. In 2002, Linda's web reveals a group of patrons who are also united in their passion for collecting twentieth-century art.

Linda MacNeil's vision is singular, bypassing many influences that appear to dominate twentieth-century studio jewelry. Her work is extremely beautiful, concentrating on form and color. Gold-plated brass is combined with geometric shapes of glass, which have been cut or cast. Color is central to the work and catches light when worn or in exhibition. There is a continuous commitment to elegance and decoration as her necklaces become socially involved through her aesthetic language. MacNeil's preferred materials are not inherently precious, but become precious as the rondelles of glass and carved elements are set like elaborate stones in the metal. Revealed through these works is Linda's constant exploration of ideas. She has examined the Art Deco period and reflected her love of nature as a source while exploring contemporary sculptural forms. Like Olaf Skoogfors and Toni Goessler-Snyder before her, she can claim to be a constructivist whose passion for geometric forms allows her to create works that are compositions in themselves—independent of the wearer. Her meticulous nature reigns as the elements are placed against the body, as seen in the photos documenting the marriage between wearer and ornament.

As an artist, MacNeil understands that jewelry is one of the most personal of all art forms; its intimate connection with the human being is inescapable. It is meant to be worn and viewed. These portraits illustrate that it also forms a visual connection between the wearer and the artist that establishes an intellectual and social identity.

One is taken back to the Paris of the 1930s when avant-garde designers created a range of jewelry that incorporated a diversity of geometric forms and colors. It was also the time when the patrons of art wore Calder and collected him, as they do MacNeil, because they were examples of unique works of art. Linda's web introduces us to a vast group of individuals who have chosen to live with her work. Their portraits emerge and document the journey of her jewelry from the studio to the secluded space and finally to the public forum, where in the words of Olaf Skoogfors, "we are provided with the human body as a gallery."[3]

—Helen W. Drutt English

---

[1] Robert Hughes, "When Beauty was Virtue," *Time*, December 24, 2001.

[2] *Man Ray's Celebrity Portrait Photographs* (New York: Dover Publications, Inc., 1995), pl. 10, 5.

[3] Daniel Marchesseau, *The Intimate World of Alexander Calder* (New York: Harry N. Abrams, 1989) p. 299, 311.

[4] *Olaf Skoogfors: 20th-Century Goldsmith 1930-1975* (Philadelphia: The Falcon Press, Inc., 1979), p. 42.

Helen W. Drutt English

Elements Necklace, 1979
acid polished aqua & red opaque glass,
14k yellow gold
6 inches diam.
with earrings
Collection Helen W. Drutt English

United in Beauty:
The Jewelry and Collectors of
Linda MacNeil

by
Suzanne Ramljak

Linda MacNeil's work has aptly been compared to that of René Lalique, who a hundred years earlier transformed the jewelry world with his innovative designs and use of materials. Although separated by a century, there are strong similarities between the two artists and it is useful to compare MacNeil's jewelry to that of the older master. Lalique is credited with revolutionizing jewelry design through his emphasis on imagination and technical virtuosity over precious materials and the imitation of past styles. Instead of concealing the setting with stones, as was traditional, Lalique used structure itself as a design element, fusing the setting and stone into a single composition. Lalique was also notable for his experiments with industrial techniques, and for his inclusion of non precious materials such as plastic and glass, which he enlisted as early as 1893. Like Lalique, MacNeil's artistic career has been marked by an ongoing commitment to innovation and experimentation. From her pioneering use of glass as a medium for contemporary jewelry, to her unorthodox treatment of industrial materials, she has continually sought new formal and technical solutions in her work. Most significantly, like her predecessor she is a master of design, producing works of great ingenuity and finesse.

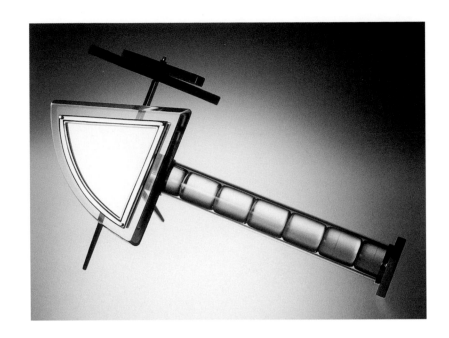

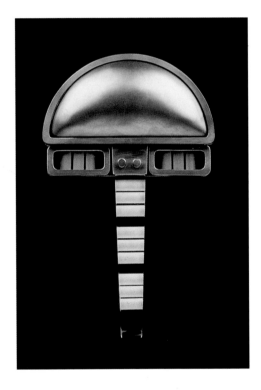

top
Hand Mirror, 1980
polished clear, orange, blue
Vitrolite glass, sterling silver
12 x 6 x 6 inches
Collection Racine Museum of Art,
donated by Brillson Foundation

bottom
Hand Mirror, 1980
cut, ground, polished clear glass, brass
12 x 6 x 2 inches
Collection Andrew & Virginia Lewis

opposite
Bronze Vessel, 1976
cast bronze, ivory, ebony details
8 x 6 x 6 inches
Private Collection

In many ways Linda MacNeil seemed destined to become a creator of beautifully designed objects. Raised in a family of creative individuals, she was exposed early on to finely wrought forms. Her own creative potential and entrepreneurial spirit emerged during high school. While still a teenager she made what she calls "hippie jewelry" that she sold for pocket money. MacNeil then progressed to creating belt buckles, which she successfully marketed on the street. These fruitful experiences with metalwork would pave the way for her enrollment in art school.

MacNeil began her studies at the Philadelphia College of Art, where she pursued her metalwork for a year before transferring to the Massachusetts College of Art. It was here that she would first encounter glass and her future husband, the artist Dan Dailey. MacNeil was introduced to glass in 1974, in a class taught by Dailey, and she has continued to find endless possibilities in this medium ever since. Although MacNeil has worked with diverse materials—including ivory, ebony, and granite—metal and glass have become the staples of her art and she has discovered many fresh ways to enhance and balance the properties of these two materials.

MacNeil's Hand Mirror series of 1980-81—begun while an undergraduate at the Rhode Island School of Design, where she received her B.F.A.—represents an early attempt to combine metal and glass in sculptural compositions. According to

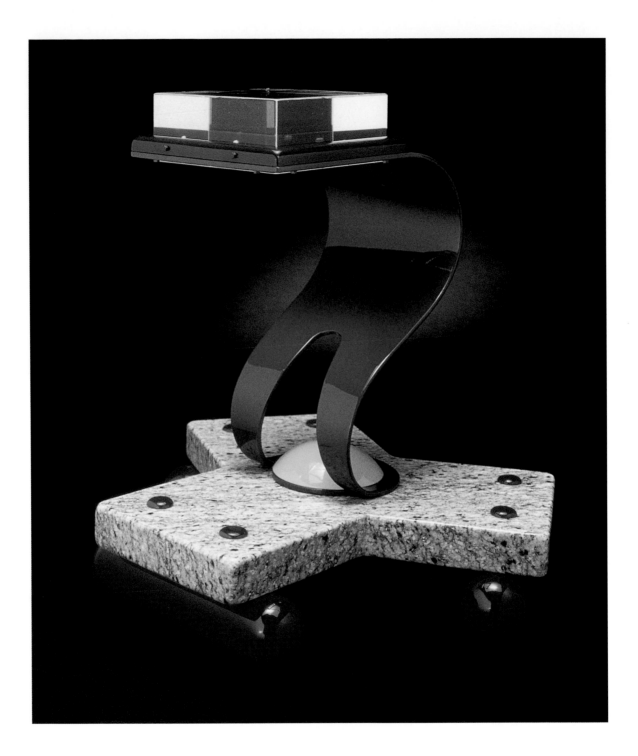

Tri-form Construction, 1988
optical glass, granite, painted brass
14 x 12 x 12 inches
Collection of the Artist

opposite
Glass Vessel, 1983
polished yellow & clear transparent
plate glass, nickle plated brass
9 x 8 x 8 inches
Private Collection

the artist these mirrors were "decorative functional objects using a sculptural approach to the designs."[1] The mirror series would be the first of many for the artist, who prefers exploring forms in a sequential manner. Her series do not unfold in a strict linear fashion, however, and she often deals with different formats and motifs simultaneously or pursues the same type of work over a number of years. Working in series has proved beneficial to both the artist's creative evolution and to the patrons of MacNeil's art, as she states "I firmly believe that you need to make twenty of something to get enough people familiar and comfortable with a concept. People enjoy some repetitiveness and yet they also expect you to grow and change. It's an ongoing challenge."[2]

In her jewelry and sculpture from the early 1980s, MacNeil exploits the creative potential of commercial plate glass in tandem with metal and stone. Metal plays a supporting role in these works, serving mainly as a connecting device for the various glass elements. Making a virtue out of a necessity, MacNeil integrates these metal rivets and screws into the final design of each piece, openly displaying the means of assembly. She has even invented some original connection designs of

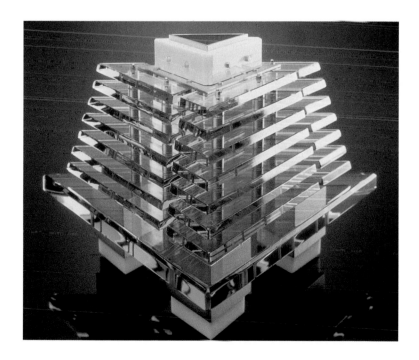

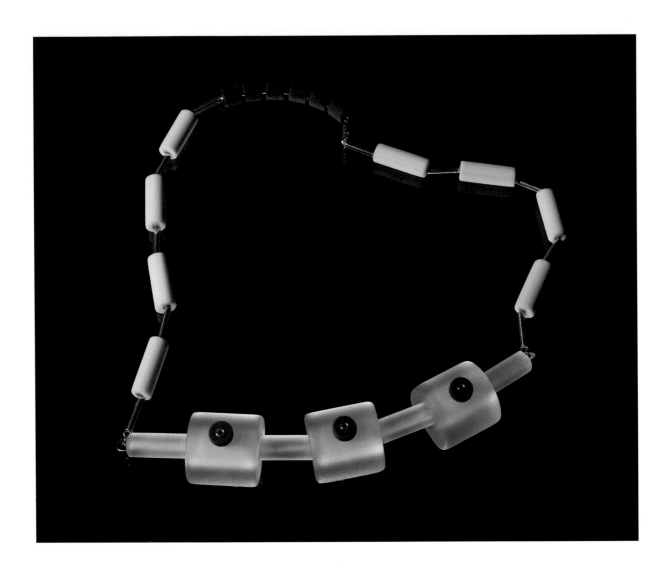

Elements Necklace, 1979
acid polished clear, light green, & red
Vitrolite glass, 14k yellow gold
6 inches diam.
Collection Victoria and Albert Museum

opposite left
Lucent Lines Necklace, 1984
acid polished & polished clear glass,
14k yellow gold tubing
7 inches diam.
Collection Joan & Jay Ochroch

opposite right
Neck Collar, 1994
acid polished purple glass, polished clear
glass, 24k gold plated brass
7 inches diam.
Collection Lynn & Jeffrey Leff

her own. The visible construction of these early necklaces and geometric sculptures reveals MacNeil's abiding interest in mechanical and architectural structures. Her sculptural vessels, in particular, display an impressive array of structural connections and a delight in intricate composition.

Not surprisingly, MacNeil points to industrial products as an inspiration for her work including bridges, street lamps, and even stainless steel bowls. She also looks to diverse historical sources such as Egyptian art, African art, Celtic art, Art Deco and Art Nouveau. Spanning the Bronze Age to the Machine Age, MacNeil's influences merge in her art to produce a timeless quality that has often been noted by admirers of her work. MacNeil's interest in historic jewelry has led her to focus on the traditional form of the neckpiece, which has become the mainstay of her creative expression.

MacNeil has devoted a number of series to the basic neckpiece format. In the Glass Elements series of the early 1980s the artist rehearses a wide variety of compositional arrangements, with multi-colored parts strung or linked together in a flexible fashion. This series also displays MacNeil's attraction to Vitrolite, a richly hued opaque glass manufactured from the 1920s into the 1940s, mainly for architectural purposes. In the Lucent Lines series, begun in the 1980s, the

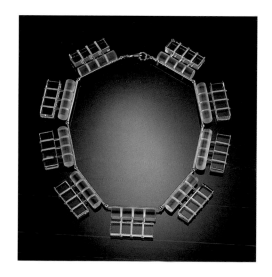

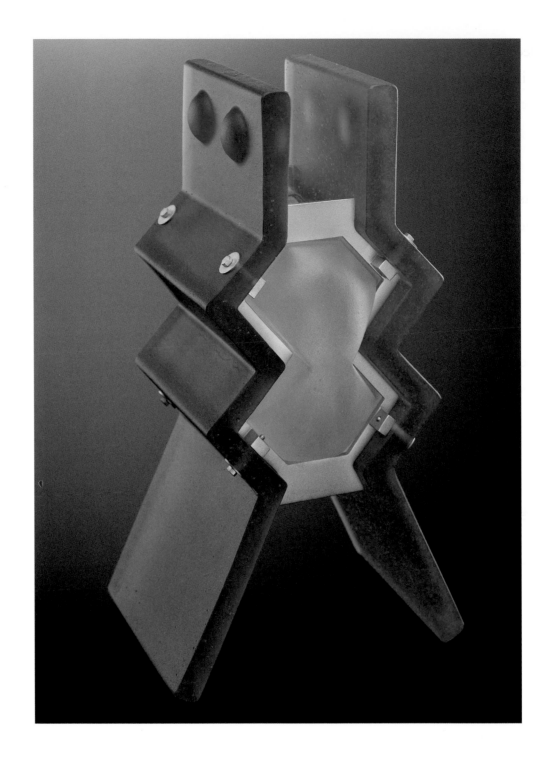

Vessel, 1981
clear, blue pâte de verre glass,
nickle plated brass
11 x 5 x 6 inches
Collection David Bernstein

opposite
Necklace, 1997
amber pâte de verre cast glass,
24k gold plated brass
6 inches diam.
Private Collection

reflective properties of glass are heightened through polishing, faceting, and even the inclusion of mirrors. Historic jewelry serves as an inspiration for this group, which is based on classic arrangements of connected components that loosely orbit the neck.

A change occurs in MacNeil's work of the late 1980s, from the freer flowing units in the Glass Elements and Lucent Lines series to the more structured forms of her Neck Collar series. For these collars, metal is enlisted as an outline for glass shapes, resulting in bold geometric compositions centered on the wearer's neck. Sporting strong contours and well-defined forms, the neck collars are some of MacNeil's most sculptural jewelry works. Without clasps and links, the functional restrictions are minimal, allowing MacNeil a greater play of inventiveness. Most of the collars are 24k gold plated brass, with the metal often treated like acid polished glass to have a similar surface texture.

In her jewelry of the mid 1990s MacNeil returned to the technique of pâte de verre, which she had explored a decade earlier in her sculptural vessels. For her Mesh Necklace series, cast glass is enlisted to achieve softened light effects, with the glass pendants hanging like glowing amulets from gold mesh rope.

Lotus Necklace, 1999
Waterford Crystal, polished clear glass, acid
polished green glass details, 18k yellow gold
6 1/2 inches diam.

A residency at the historic crystal factory in Waterford, Ireland led to the Waterford Crystal series of 1998-99. Instead of the icy coldness and sharp facets often found in lead crystal pieces, MacNeil produced works with warmth and subtle radiance. She also introduced more organic elements into her designs like the recurrent lotus form along with gently flowing contours. The Waterford works signal a shift in MacNeil's creative evolution from the geometric and architectonic to the more organic; from angles to curves. The growing curvaceousness in her works was inspired in part by the dynamic forms of nature. As MacNeil explains, "My style in the past was quite geometric, based on architecture and mechanical connections. I have evolved toward a more organic feeling in design. Part of this is a respect for nature. When you look at nature it is not rigid. But I still enjoy simplicity and geometry. Even under the curve there is order." Her newfound appreciation of organic form is potently evident in MacNeil's Floral Series of 2001.

MacNeil is rare in her ability to combine the refined planning and composition of a designer with the diligent labor and personal devotion of a craftsperson. Like craftspeople of past centuries, she approaches her work with a total immersion of self, remaining oblivious to time in the pursuit of perfect form. This investment directly translates into the quality of her work. MacNeil recognizes the difficulty of remaining so focused in our modern world and is attracted to historical jewelry for its superior workmanship, "I am much more interested in the quality of work of the past," she says. "It is more magical. I think the pace of life these days has really watered things down. In the past there were so many more craftsmen and they were trained to see things that people don't see now." MacNeil's undaunted quest for perfection, in spite of modern diversions and short-cuts, sets her apart from most other artists in the field of jewelry today.

Linda MacNeil's dedication to her craft is fueled by a genuine love and appreciation for her chosen material. She revels in the mercurial properties of glass: it can be clear, translucent, or opaque; the surfaces can appear shiny and

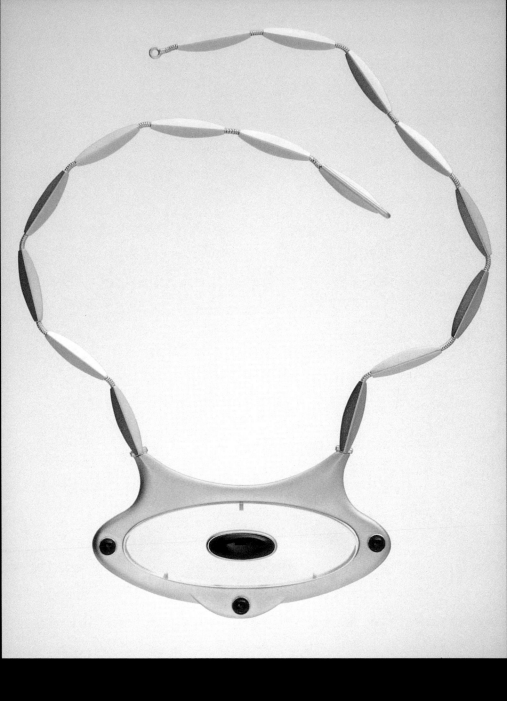

Exotic Pea Pod Floral Necklace, 2001
acid polished, polished clear glass, polished black
Vitrolite glass, onyx details, 24k gold plated brass
pendant 3 inches
with earrings

many other artist-jewelers, she is committed to wearability as the primary function of jewelry. Her winning formula combines beauty and usefulness in perfect accord. To insure that the jewelry is indeed wearer friendly, MacNeil wears all the pieces around the studio to test out their sensation and movement. "It is going to feel right by the time I am finished with it," she declares.

While she strives to create a comfortable and enjoyable wearing experience for the owner, MacNeil's work is not for everyone and poses a subtle challenge to potential buyers. Because she uses glass and gold plated brass—mainly for the creative freedom these materials allow—collectors must appreciate her work for its beauty and design quality versus the intrinsic value of the materials. Instead of investing in costly substances, they are knowingly paying for an original design concept. As MacNeil has stated, "they understand that they are buying the artwork not the materials."

With other mediums like painting, this expectation of material value does not apply, but with jewelry—given its close association with portable wealth and the use of precious metal and stones—it is harder to break the mental habit, especially since MacNeil's works have the semblance of gems and pure gold. Whereas glass jewels had value and prestige in antiquity, they have lost much of this importance in contemporary culture. From its first invention in the second millennium BC, glass served as a material for adornment, used for beads and small ornaments. Although the appreciation of glass adornment has survived over the centuries— and was brilliantly revived by the late nineteenth-century jewelry of Lalique—glass has retained a second-class status to gems and other precious stones. But decreased market value does not mean lesser artistic value, and aesthetic worth is what MacNeil strives for and achieves in her work. The group of women who have chosen to acquire and wear MacNeil's works are exceptional in their ability to appreciate the artistry in her designs, and reveal a strong degree of discernment and vision.

Other than their shared appreciation for MacNeil's work, the collectors of her jewelry comprise a diverse group of individuals. While they are all necessarily women, frequently it is the men in their lives who have purchased the works that they wear. The women's collecting interests range from antiques to contemporary art and many have a specialty in glass collecting. Some collect the work of other contemporary jewelers, while others do not. They come from assorted professional backgrounds and have varying degrees of involvement in the art world, including serving as critics, artists, docents, photographers, dealers, and museum board members.

MacNeil has speculated on the common denominator within the group of women who buy and enjoy her jewelry, stating, "They enjoy the beauty and the quality of the pieces, and feel proud that they found something special. The collector has a talent as well as an artist to seek out interesting things. You have to give them credit for choosing such a piece. All of us have an interest in being unique in some way."

This desire to distinguish oneself from the crowd and declare one's uniqueness is an essential element in a collector's attraction to MacNeil's work, as it is with most one-of-a-kind objects. In the case of jewelry, unlike other handcrafted objects, the identification between owner and piece is even more intimate. Because the object is worn on one's person, the wearer and the work become identified with each other to a greater degree. As jewelry calls attention to itself, it is also brings attention to the wearer, adding instant value and interest. The collecting of jewelry is unique in this way, due to the strong fusion of possession and possessed.

In his provocative book, *Collecting, An Unruly Passion*, Werner Muensterberger argues that all collecting fulfills certain emotional needs, many rooted in our childhood. He writes, "the ownership of objects and the pride and pleasure in their possession has more than one function: the object becomes a countermeasure to insecurity…. It also conveys the owner's covert need to hear pronouncements of praise and admiration."[3] He goes on to suggest that the objects we collect provide a culturally acceptable means of asserting ourselves and declaring our specialness and worthiness.[4]

Whether or not one follows Muensterberger's argument in its entirety, there is some truth to his explanation of the collector's motives. Comments by the owners of MacNeil's jewelry underline similar reasons for collecting and wearing her work. Whether or not the satisfaction is rooted in the fulfillment of childhood needs, all receive a gratifying amount of admiration and praise when they don MacNeil's jewelry. When questioned about how they feel when they are wearing her work, they repeatedly comment on feeling "attractive," "elegant," "confident," "authoritative," and "special."[5] There is an unabashed pleasure in receiving attention from friends and strangers alike.

In the same way that an owner and her jewelry become merged in the process of wearing a piece, there is a coalescing of the artist and her work in the process of creating it. Thus, to wear a piece by Linda MacNeil is to wear a part of her. This realization was also expressed by several collectors of MacNeil's works who know and admire the person behind the art. Appropriately, to wear a piece of the artist is literally to wear beauty, since in Latin the name Linda means beautiful or pretty. Like links in a chain, the artist, her creations, and her collectors have become intricately united in beauty.

—Suzanne Ramljak

---

[1] Karen Chambers, "Linda MacNeil: A Detailed Look," *Metalsmith*, Summer 1996, Vol. 16/No. 3, p. 27.

[2] Unless otherwise noted, all artist quotes are from an interview with the author, September 17, 2000.

[3] Werner Muensterberger, *Collecting: An Unruly Passion, Psychological Perspectives*, (Princeton NJ: Princeton University Press, 1994), p. 254.

[4] Ibid, p. 255.

[5] Drawn from responses to a questionnaire completed by collectors of MacNeil's jewelry.

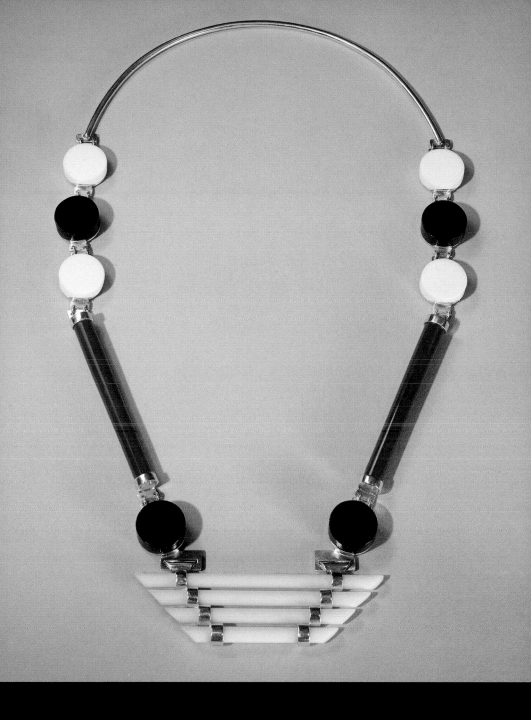

Elements Necklace, 1979

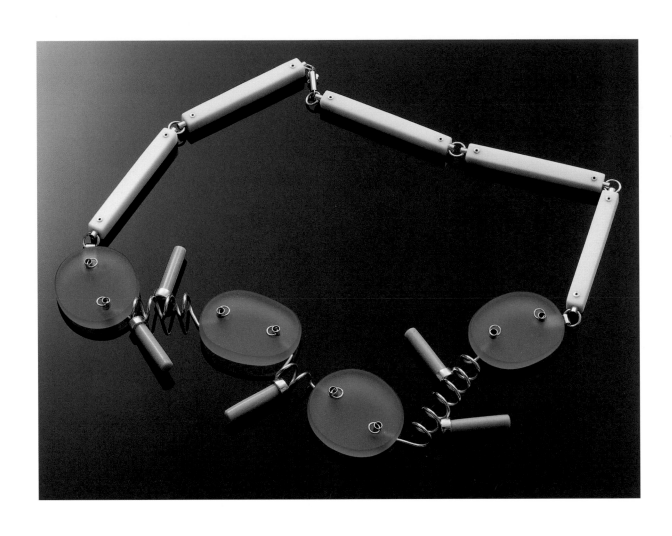

Elements Necklace, 1980
acid polished transparent blue glass, polished
cream & tan Vitrolite glass, 14k yellow gold
6 inches diam.
Collection Smithsonian American Art Museum,
donated by Vera & Dr. Robert Loeffler

Barbara Tarleton Tricebock

Sterling Silver Necklace, 1977
ivory & ebony detail
pendant: 3 inches
with earrings
Collection of the Artist

Elements Necklace, 1979
polished black, white, light green, & red
Vitrolite glass, 14k yellow gold
necklace 6 inches diam.
bracelet 3 inches diam.
Collection Anne & Ron Abramson

Ruth Dean, Ph.D.

Elements Necklace, 1980
polished maroon & cream Vitrolite glass, 14k yellow gold
6 inches diam.
with earrings
Collection Dr. Ruth Dean & Andrew Dean

Elements Necklace, 1983
polished opaque orange glass, polished
transparent yellow glass, 14k yellow gold
7 inches diam.
Collection Anne & Ron Abramson

Dorothy R. Saxe

Elements Necklace, 1982
acid polished transparent red glass, polished
light blue crystal, 14k yellow gold
6 inches diam.
with earrings
Collection Dorothy & George Saxe

Susie Shapiro

Elements Necklace, 1983
acid polished clear glass, polished blue, green,
red, purple & orange glass, 14k yellow gold tubing
6 inches diam.
with earrings
Collection Susie Shapiro & Andrew Magdanz

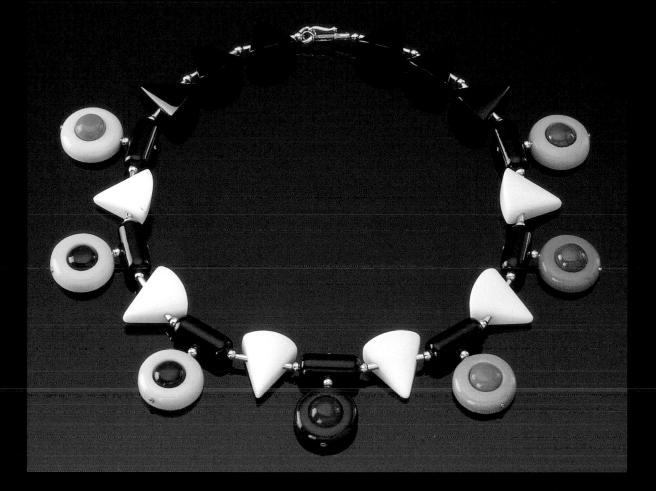

Elements Necklace, 1984
polished black, white, & multicolored
Vitrolite glass, 14k yellow gold
6 inches diam.
Private Collection

Susie Cushner

Elements Necklace, 1984
acid polished clear glass, polished black,
white & multicolored Vitrolite glass
14k yellow gold
9 inches diam.
with earrings
Collection Susie Cushner

opposite
Elements Necklace, 1984
acid polished black, polished
white & multicolored Vitrolite glass,
14k yellow gold
8 inches diam.
Collection Anne & Ron Abramson

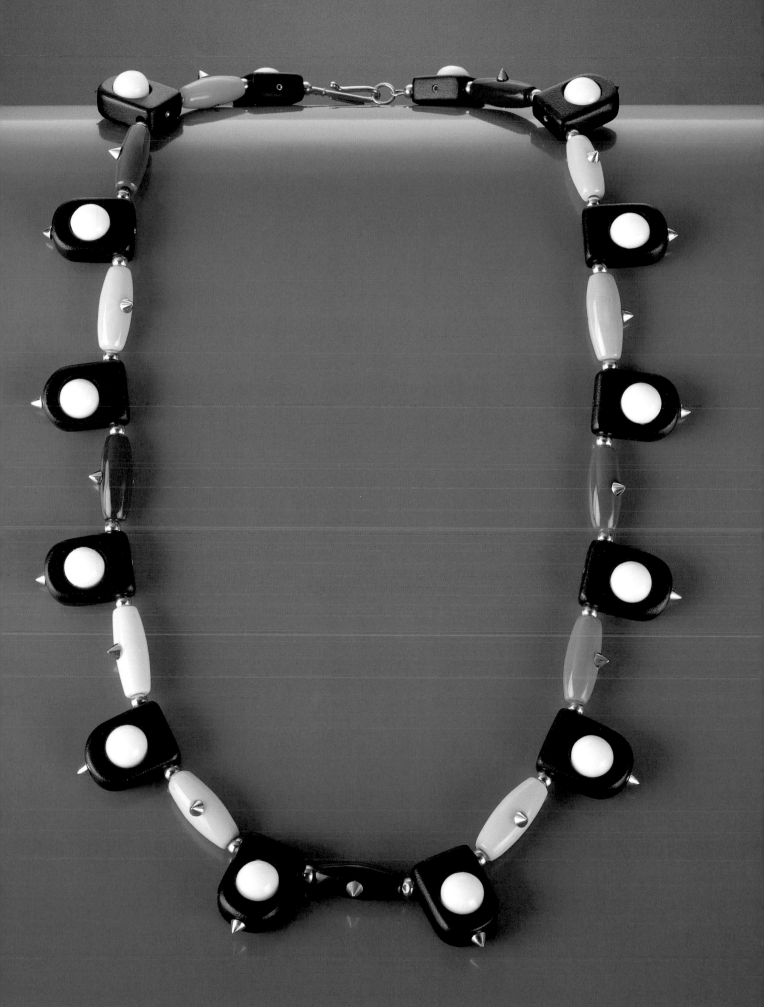

Libby Hoffman

Elements Necklace, 1993
acid polished opaque black glass,
transparent green cast glass,
14k yellow gold, 24k gold plated brass
6 inches diam.
Collection Libby & Burton Hoffman

Lois Boardman

Elements Necklace, 1984
acid polished clear cast glass, polished
multicolored Vitrolite glass, 14k yellow gold
9 inches diam.
Collection Boardman Family

Nancy MacNeil

Elements Necklace, 1985
polished clear glass, polished granite & lapis,
14k yellow gold
9 inches diam.
with earrings
Collection Nancy MacNeil

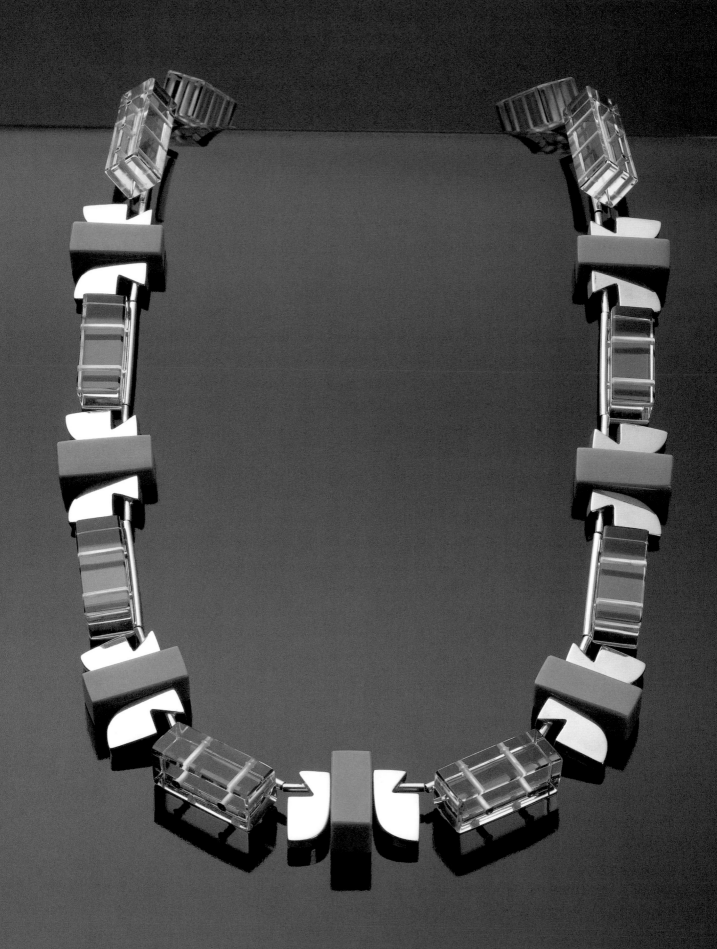

Myrna B. Palley

opposite
Lucent Lines Necklace, 1982
polished clear glass, polished orange
Vitrolite glass, sterling silver
8 inches diam.
Private Collection

Lucent Lines Necklace, 1983
polished blue, yellow & clear glass, polished
clear glass, 14k yellow gold tubing
7 inches diam.
Collection Myrna & Sheldon Palley

Lynn Leff

opposite
Neck Collar, 1988
acid polished smoky gray glass,
red painted brass
7 inches diam.
Collection of the Artist

Neck Collar, 1994
acid polished purple glass, polished
clear glass, 24k gold plated brass
7 inches diam.
with earrings
Collection Lynn & Jeffrey Leff

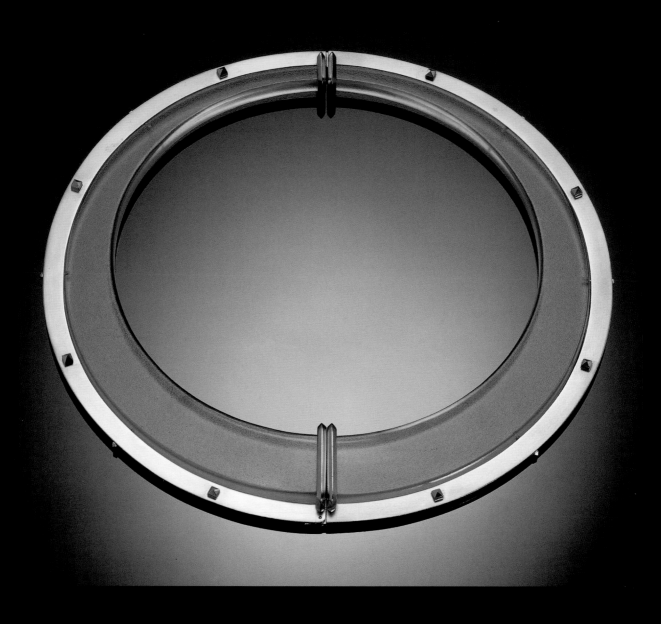

Neck Collar, 1988
acid polished transparent yellow glass,
24k gold plated brass
6 inches diam.
Collection of the Artist

Marcia Emerson

Neck Collar, 1988
acid polished & polished optical glass, green
painted brass detail, 24k gold plated brass
7 inches width
with earrings
Collection Marcia & Mark Emerson

Jane Cotter

Neck Collar, 1994
acid polished blue glass, polished pink
mirrored glass, 24k gold plated brass
7 inches diam.
with earrings
Collection of the Artist & Jane Cotter

Daphne Farago

Neck Collar, 1998
acid polished purple glass, polished
clear mirrored glass detail, 24k gold
plated brass
6 1/2 inches diam.
with earrings
Collection Daphne & Peter Farago
Foundation

opposite
Neck Collar, 1990
acid polished clear glass, acid polished
lilac triangular glass elements, 24k gold
plated brass with red painted detail
8 x 5 3/4 x 2 1/4 inches
with earrings
Collection American Craft Museum

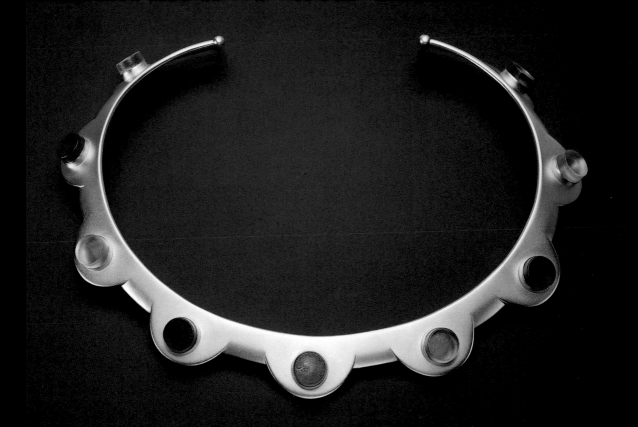

Becky Benaroya

Neck Collar, 1995
acid polished clear glass, polished clear
mirrored glass detail, 24k gold plated brass
6 1/2 inches diam.
with earrings
Collection Becky & Jack Benaroya

Joan Chodorkoff, Ph.D.

Neck Collar, 1988
polished clear optical glass,
24k gold plated brass
pendant 1 1/2 inches square
Collection Drs. Joan & Bernard
Chodorkoff

opposite
Neck Collar, 1986
acid polished multicolored glass,
24k gold plated brass
7 inches diam.
with earrings & bracelet
Collection Corning Museum of Glass, 1991

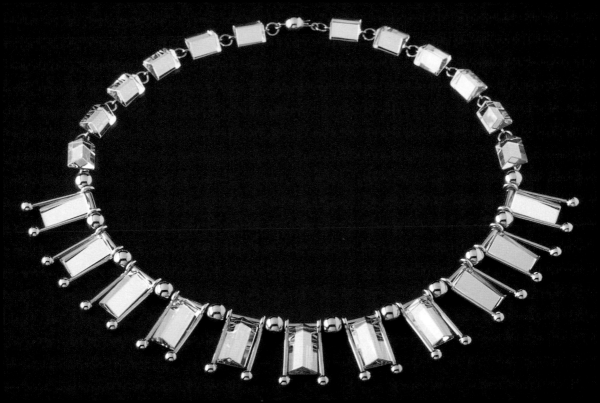

Barbara Carpenter

Mirrored Glass Necklace, 1995
polished clear mirrored glass, 14k yellow gold
7 inches diam.
with earrings
Collection Barbara & Harlow Carpenter

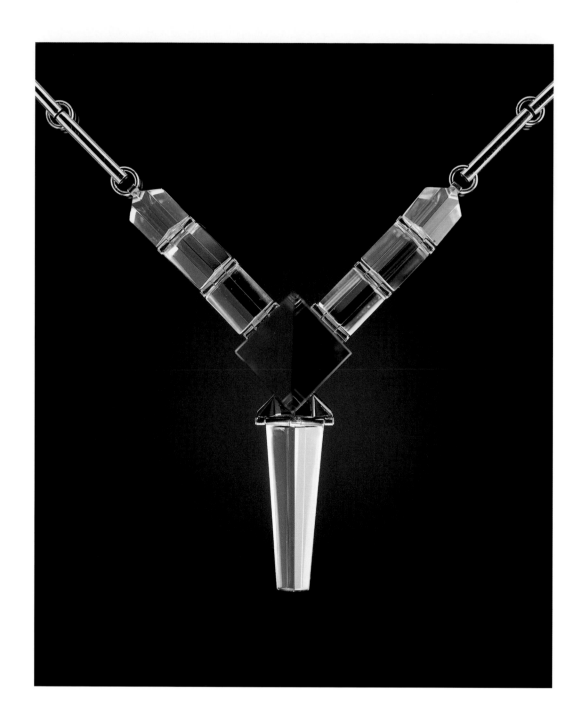

Mirrored Glass Necklace, 2001
polished laminated clear & blue glass, polished
clear mirrored glass, polished black Vitrolite
glass, polished 14k yellow gold
pendant 3 inches
with earrings
Collection Tracy & Joe Kross

Anna Mendel

Mirrored Glass Necklace, 1995
polished mirrored clear glass, 14k yellow gold
7 inches diam.
wIth earrings
Collection Anna & Joseph Mendel

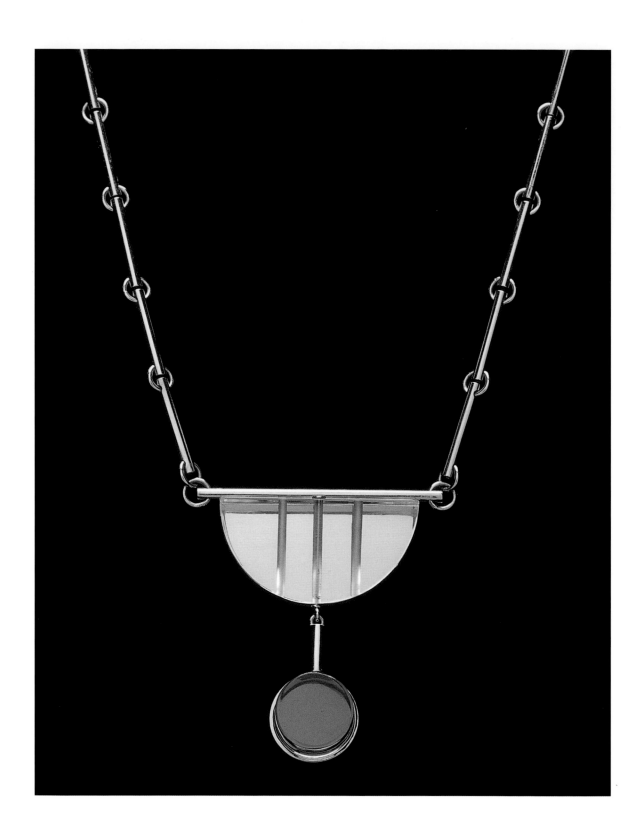

Julie Lewis, M.D.

opposite
Lucent Lines Necklace, 1995
polished transparent clear & blue glass,
14k yellow gold
pendant 2 inches
with earrings
Collection Dr. Julie Lewis

Susie Jacobson

previous
Lucent Lines Necklace, 1993
Polished clear, blue & yellow transparent
glass, 14k yellow gold tubing
6 inches diam.
with earrings
Collection Susie & Scott Jacobson

Lucent Lines Necklace, 1995
polished clear, pink, blue, yellow,
& green transparent glass, sterling
silver tubing
6 inches diam.
with earrings
Collection Susie & Scott Jacobson

opposite
Lucent Lines Necklace, 1994
acid polished clear glass, 14k yellow
gold tubing
6 inches diam.
with earrings
Collection Marcia & Mark Emerson

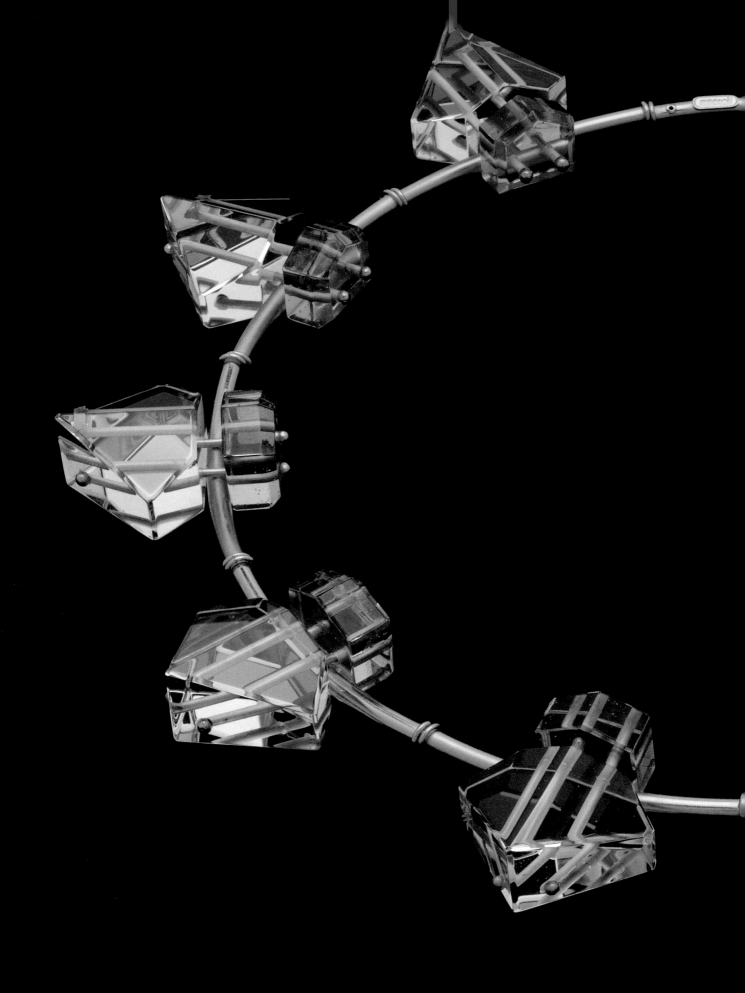

Joan Ochroch

opposite detail
Lucent Lines Necklace, 1994
polished clear & neodymium glass,
14k yellow gold tubing, 24k gold plated
7 inches diam.
with earrings
Collection Joan & Jay Ochroch

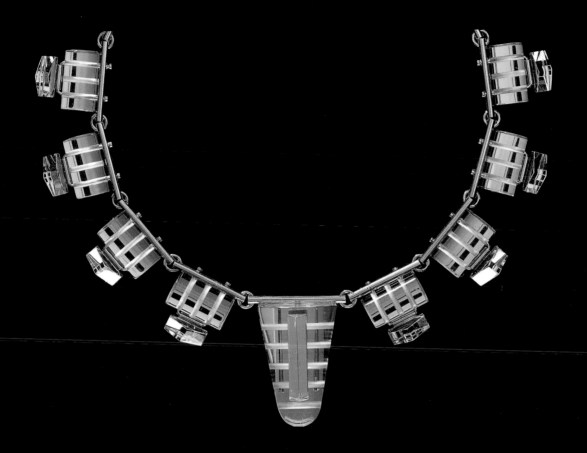

opposite
Lucent Lines Necklace, 1983
acid polished smoky gray & brown
transparent glass, 14k yellow gold tubing
9 inches diam.
with earrings
Collection Joan & Jay Ochroch

Lucent Lines Necklace, 2002
polished clear optical glass, mirrored glass
detail, 14k yellow gold
7 inches diam.
with earrings
Collection Nanette Laitman

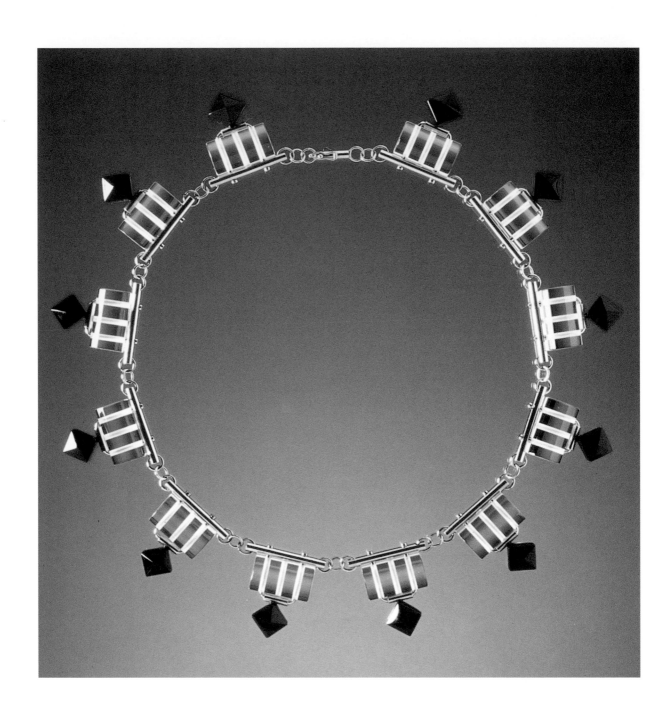

Lucent Lines Necklace, 1999
polished clear optical glass, polished red glass,
14k yellow gold
6 1/2 inches diam.
with earrings
Collection Sharon & Jon Kuhn

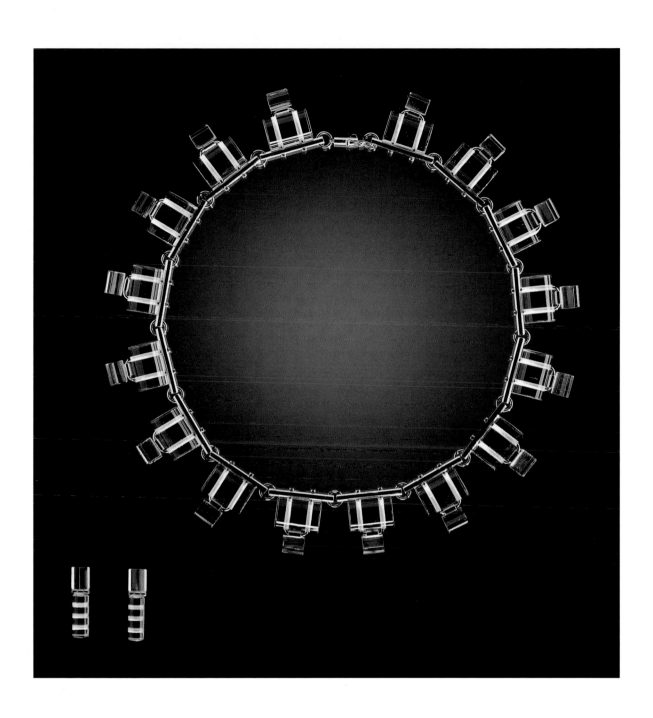

Lucent Lines Necklace, 2001
polished clear optical glass, polished light
blue glass details, 14k yellow gold
7 inches diam.
with earrings

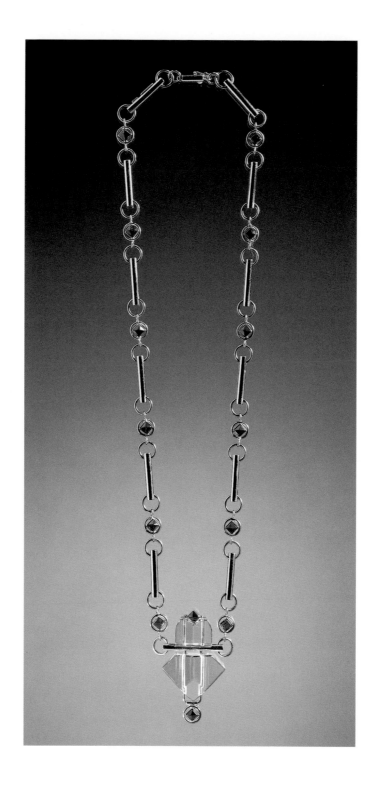

Lucent Lines Necklace, 1999
polished transparent clear glass,
polished purple glass, polished
14k yellow gold
pendant 1 1/2 inches
with earrings

opposite
Lucent Lines Necklace, 2000
polished clear optical glass, polished
clear mirrored glass details,
14k yellow gold
7 inches diam.
with earrings
Collection of the Artist

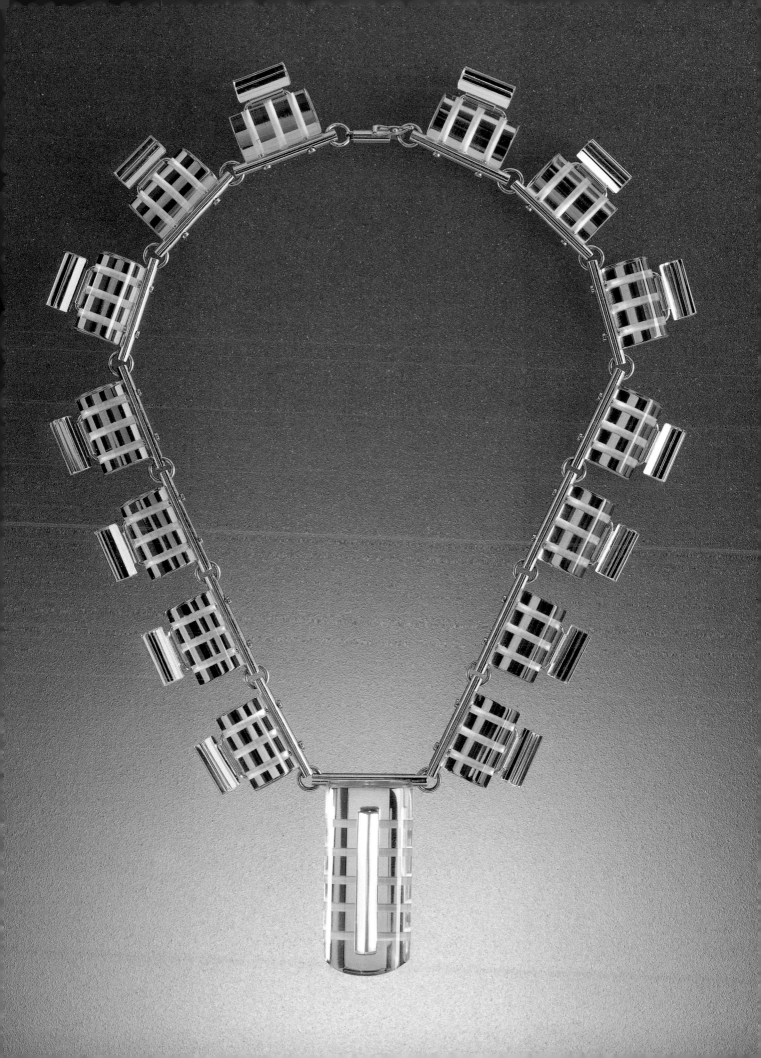

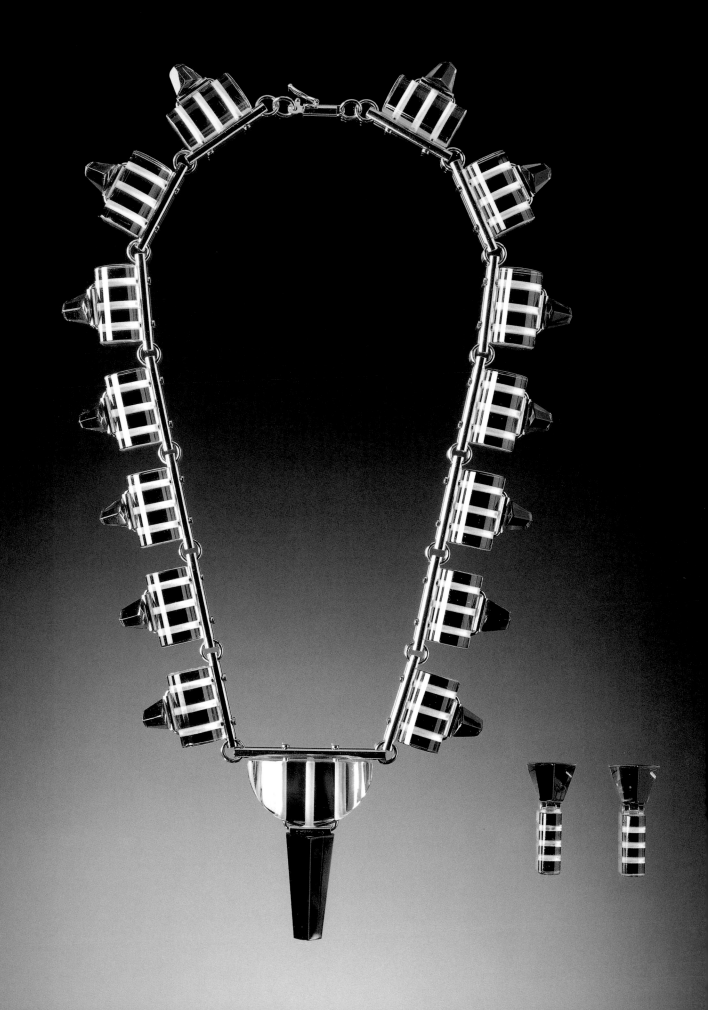

Chris Rifkin

opposite
Lucent Lines Necklace, 2000
polished clear optical glass, polished purple
glass details, 14k yellow gold
7 inches diam.
with earrings
Collection Drs. Arlene & Norman Silvers

Lucent Lines Necklace, 1992
polished smoky gray & clear glass,
14k yellow gold tubing
8 inches diam.
Collection Chris Rifkin

Robin Glancy

Capsule Necklace, 1990
acid polished brown & dark green glass,
14k gold plated brass
6 inches diam.
Collection Robin & Michael Glancy

opposite
Capsule Necklace, 1990
polished gray, black & white granite,
blue & red painted details,
24k gold plated brass details
6 inches diam.
with bracelet
Collection Anne & Ron Abramson

polished, or textured and dull; it lends itself to a wide range of color effects and its potential for luminosity is unbounded. MacNeil's glass repertoire includes plate glass, cast glass, Vitrolite, and crystal, and her understanding of the medium has allowed her to make this common material perform numerous design feats. MacNeil feels that she is nowhere near exhausting the potential of glass as an artistic medium. "Glass is very difficult and there are a lot of problems and challenges with it," she affirms. "It is a material with so many different characters, it can go on forever. My little time span exploring glass is nothing compared to what's possible."

MacNeil's work also communicates an irresistible sense of delight in the creative process and in the discovery of new design possibilities. "Challenge" is a recurring word in MacNeil's discussion of her work, and she views new artistic trials as something positive, whether it be an unusual commission or an untried approach to jewelry construction.

Whichever technique MacNeil employs, she masterfully choreographs the play of solid metal and evanescent glass, structure and light, coolness and warmth. She is a designer of light as well as of form in her works and there is a built in luminosity that radiates out from each piece. Like the fabled King Midas with his golden touch, she has the power to transform glass into gemstones and base metal into precious material. Her lapidary approach to glass has yielded "jewels" that rival nature's splendor in their color and light.

Along with her ongoing quest for perfection, MacNeil has remained committed to making what she calls "user friendly" jewelry that is comfortable and pleasurable to wear. Unlike other objects, jewelry is intended to be worn, and only becomes complete when it is on a human body. Regardless of how bold MacNeil's jewelry designs become, they are always attuned to the wearer's experience of the object. Instead of making unwearable or impractical works, as do

Charlotte Heil

Elements Necklace, 1983
acid polished transparent green cast glass,
polished black & white Vitrolite glass,
14k yellow gold
6 inches diam.
Collection Charlotte Heil

Johanna Rice

Capsule Necklace, 1988
acid polished cobalt blue glass, 14k gold plated brass
6 inches diam.
Collection Johanna Rice

The Honorable MeraLee Goldman

Capsule Necklace, 1990
acid polished clear glass, 14k gold plated brass
6 inches diam.
Collection MeraLee & Leonard Goldman

Sophie Walter-Zoll

Capsule Necklace, 1988
Polished light blue glass,
nickle-plated brass
6 inches diam.
Collection Sophia Walter & Stuart Zoll

opposite
Capsule Necklace, 1988
acid polished clear glass,
red painted brass
6 inches diam.
Collection of the Artist

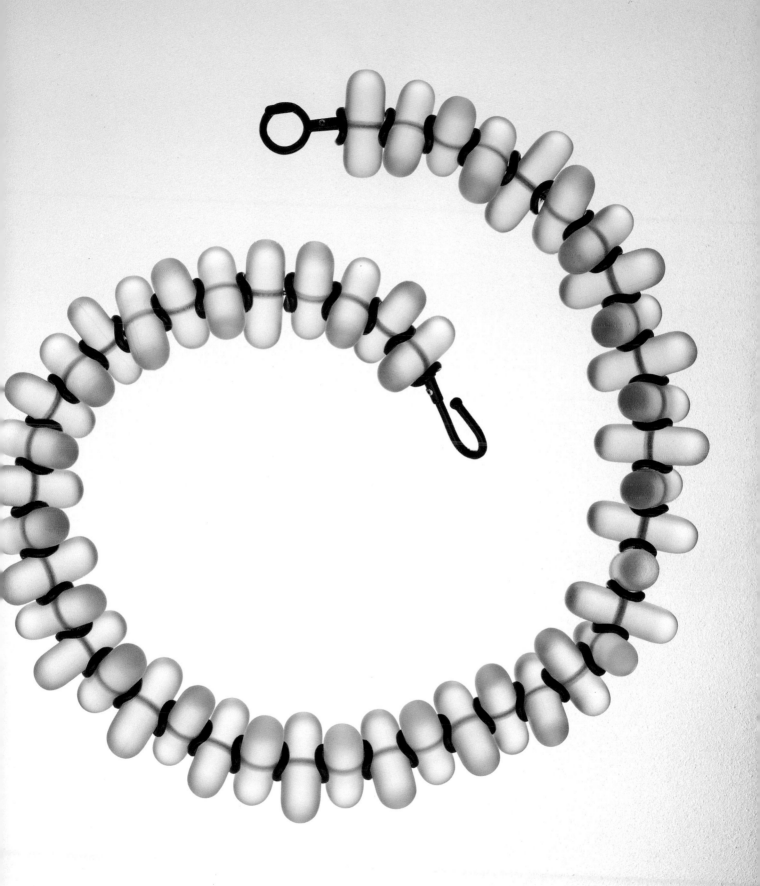

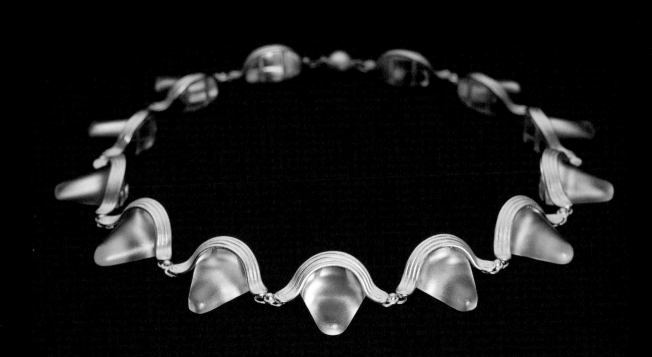

Colleen Kollar-Kotelly

opposite
Ram's Horn Necklace, 1995
acid polished clear glass,
24k gold plated sterling silver
7 inches diam.
Collection Colleen & John Kotelly

Ram's Horn Necklace, 1998
polished clear optical glass,
24k gold plated sterling silver
6 inches diam.
Collection Boston Museum of Fine Arts

Judy Rosenburg

Tri-Mesh Necklace, 1998
polished amber glass, 24k gold plated brass
pendant 2 inches
Collection Judy & Ira Rosenberg

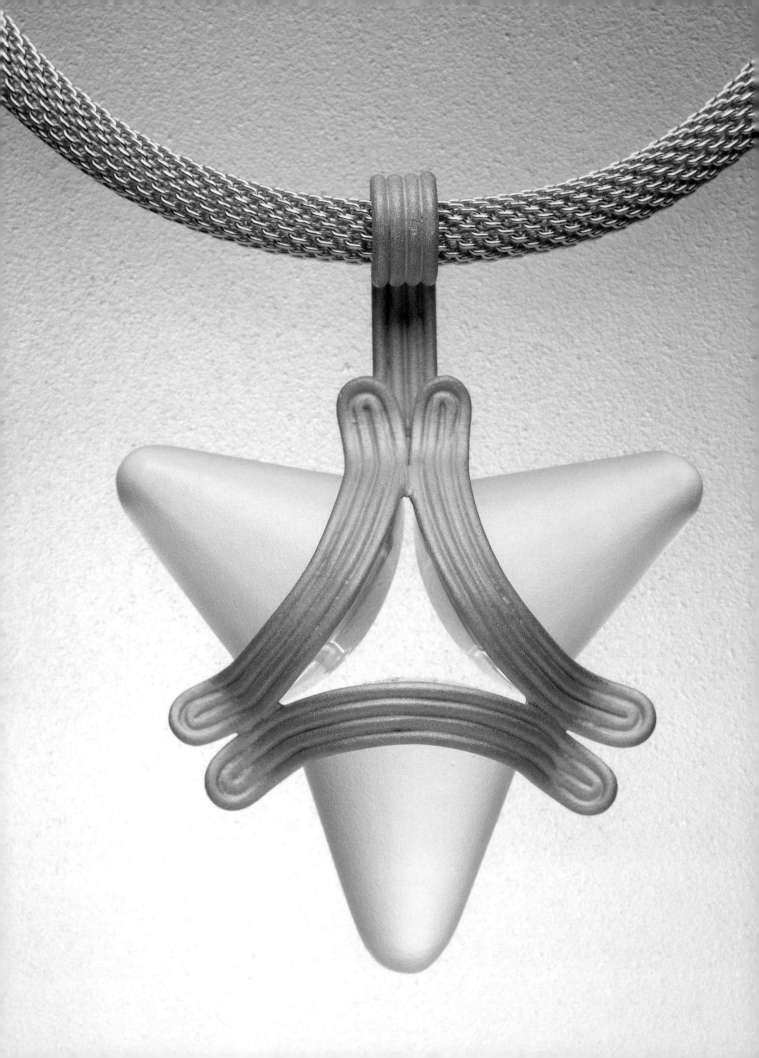

Judith A. Mayfield

opposite
Tri-Mesh Necklace, 1997
acid polished clear glass, 24k gold plated brass
pendant 2 inches
Collection Myrtle S. & Dr. Cyrus Katzen

Tri-Mesh Necklace, 1998
polished clear lead crystal, 24k gold plated brass
pendant 2 inches
Collection Judith A. Mayfield & Richard Burge

Ram's Horn Brooch, 1998
acid polished clear glass, polished black
Vitrolite glass detail, 24k gold plated brass
3 3/4 inches
Collection Anna & Joseph Mendel

Carolyn Simons

Ram's Head Mesh Necklace, 1998
acid polished clear glass, polished clear
mirrored glass detail, 24k gold plated brass
pendant 2 inches
with earrings
Collection Carolyn Simons

Mimi Dunn

Ram's Head Mesh Necklace, 1999
acid polished yellow glass, polished amber
glass detail, 24k gold plated brass
pendant 3 3/4 inches
with earrings
Collection Mimi Dunn & Ronald Shapiro

Carol Parven Hutter and Daisy

Ram's Head Mesh Necklace, 1999
acid polished yellow tinted glass, polished
green glass detail, 24k gold plated brass
pendant 2 inches
Collection Carol Parven Hutter & Sid Hutter

Phyllis Poplawski

Ram's Head Mesh Necklace, 1998
polished blue tinted optical glass,
polished clear mirrored glass detail,
24k gold plated brass
pendant/brooch 2 inches
Collection Phyllis & Ruben Poplawski

Liz Beers Sandler

Ram's Head Mesh Necklace, 1998
acid polished clear glass, polished light green
glass detail, 24k gold plated brass
pendant 2 inches
with earrings
Collection Elizabeth Beers Sandler & Norman Sandler

Natalie Werbitt

opposite
Ram's Horn Mesh Necklace, 1998
acid polished clear glass, polished purple glass detail,
24k gold plated brass
pendant 3 3/4 inches
Collection Natalie & Dr. Warren Werbitt

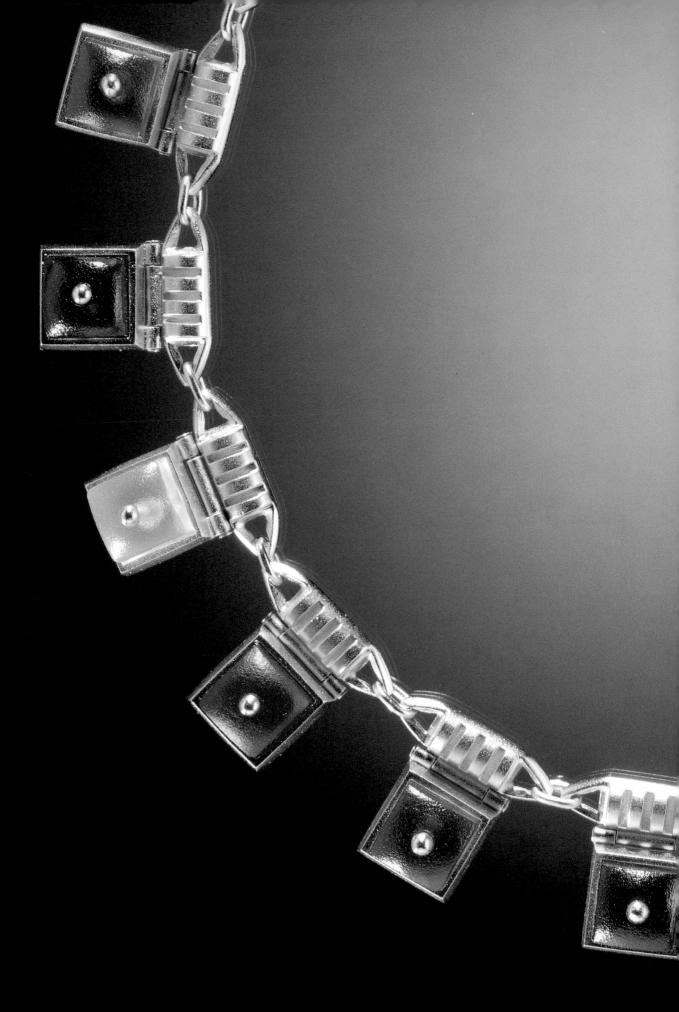

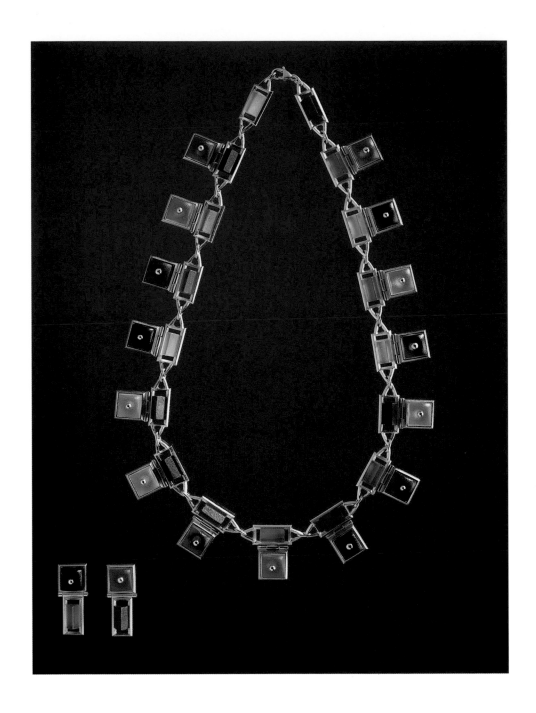

previous
Fanfare Nexus Necklace, 2001
acid polished transparent multicolored glass,
24k gold plated brass
7 inches diam.
with earrings
Collection Chris Rifkin

Jubilee Nexus Necklace, 2001
acid polished transparent multicolored
glass, 24k gold plated brass
6 1/2 inches diam.
with earrings
Collection Muriel Myerson

opposite
Rainbow Nexus Necklace, 2001
acid polished clear & multicolored glass,
24k gold plated brass
6 1/2 inches diam.
with earrings
Collection MeraLee & Leonard Goldman

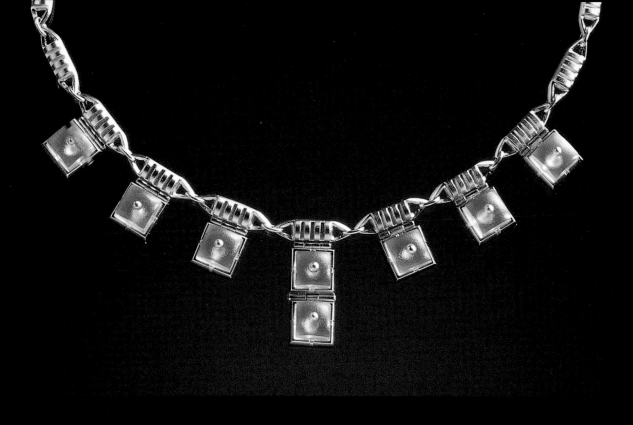

Geometric Steller Nexus Necklace, 1999
acid polished clear glass, 24k gold plated brass
7 inches diam.

Anne B. Cohen

Latropolis Nexus Necklace, 2000
acid polished yellow tinted glass, polished black
Vitrolite glass, 24k gold plated brass
6 inches diam.
pendant 3 inches
with earrings
Collection Anne & Marvin Cohen

Jenifer Schermer

opposite
Black Diamond Nexus Necklace, 1999
polished tinted yellow glass, polished opaque
black Vitrolite glass, 24k gold plated brass
7 inches diam.
pendant 4 inches
with earrings
Collection Joan & Milton Baxt

Susan Crowell

opposite
Rhombus Fantasy Nexus Necklace, 2000
polished transparent purple, yellow tinted, & amber
glass, 24k gold plated brass
pendant 4 inches
with earrings

Deco Night Nexus Necklace, 2000
polished black & amber glass, 24k gold plated brass
pendant 4 inches
with earrings
Collection Susan & Dr. Ronald Crowell

Amye Price Gumbinner

opposite
Blue Velvet Nexus Necklace, 2000
acid polished clear glass, polished transparent blue glass,
24k gold plated brass
pendant 2 inches
with earrings
Collection Amye Price Gumbinner & Paul S. Gumbinner

Mesh Necklace, 1995
polished multicolored glass, 24k gold plated brass
6 inches diam.
with earrings
Collection Nicole Keulers-Beijer & Gert Beijer

Emily Gurtman

Mesh Necklace, 1996
acid polished multicolored glass, 24k gold plated brass
6 inches diam.
with earrings
Collection Emily & Dr. Fred Gurtman

Barbara Handler First

opposite
Mesh Necklace, 1998
polished clear, red & blue glass,
polished clear mirrored glass detail,
24k gold plated brass
pendant 3 inches
with earrings
Collection Barbara & Howard First

Mimi S. Livingston

Mesh Necklace, 1998
polished pink tinted glass, polished blue glass,
mirror detail, 24k gold plated brass
pendant 3 inches
Collection Mimi S. Livingston

Carolyn J. Springborn

Mesh Necklace, 1997
polished tinted yellow glass, polished green
glass detail, 24k gold plated brass
pendant 3 inches
with earrings
Collection Carolyn J. & Robert Springborn

Jan Schrier Streicher, D.V.M.

opposite
Mesh Necklace, 1998
acid polished clear glass, polished blue glass,
24k gold plated brass
pendant 3 inches
with earrings
Collection Drs. Jan & Michael Streicher

Mimi Rieder

Mesh Necklace, 1996
polished transparent clear and green glass,
24k gold plated brass
pendant 2 inches
with earrings
Collection Mimi & Robert Rieder

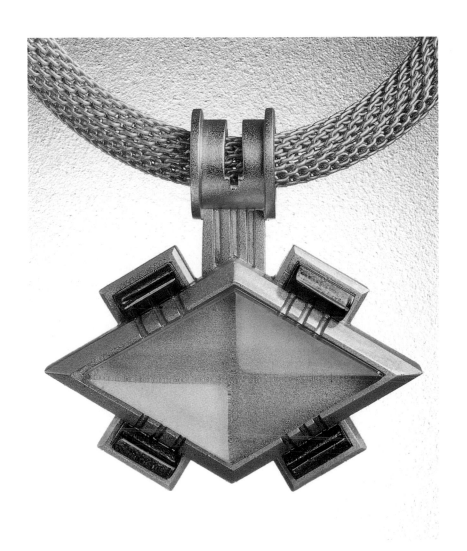

Mesh Necklace, 1998
polished yellow tinted glass, polished purple
glass detail, 24k gold plated brass
pendant 3 inches
with earrings
Collection Robin & Allan Klein

Sharon Oleksiak

Mesh Necklace, 1998
polished purple glass, onyx detail,
24k gold plated brass, 14k gold
pendant 2 inches
with earrings
Collection Sharon Oleksiak & Steven Weinburg

Janice Lyle, Ph.D.

Mesh Necklace, 1996
polished transparent green glass,
24k gold plated brass
pendant 1 inch
with earrings
Collection Janice Lyle

Mesh Necklace, 1996
polished clear and opaque black Vitrolite glass,
24k gold plated brass
pendant 2 inches
with earrings
Collection Barbara & Dr. Richard Basch

Dale Anderson
Bruce Pepich

opposite
Mesh Necklace, 1995
acid polished green pâte de verre glass, polished clear
mirrored glass detail, 24k gold plated brass
pendant 2 inches
Collection Racine Museum of Art,
donated by Dale & Doug Anderson, 1998

Dorothy J. Paul

Mesh Necklace, 1995
acid polished green pâte de verre glass,
polished clear mirrored glass detail,
24k gold plated brass
pendant 1 1/2 inches
Collection Dorothy & Orval Paul

Joan W. Harris

Mesh Necklace, 1995
acid polished transparent green pâte de verre glass,
24k gold plated brass
pendant 3 inches
Collection Joan W. & Irving Harris

June Dubrowsky

opposite
Mesh Necklace, 1998
acid polished green pâte de verre glass,
polished clear mirrored glass detail,
24k gold plated brass
pendant 3 inches
with earrings
Collection June & Dr. Fred Dubrowsky

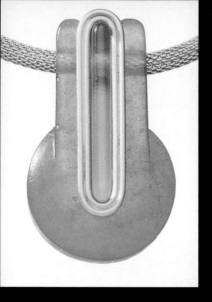

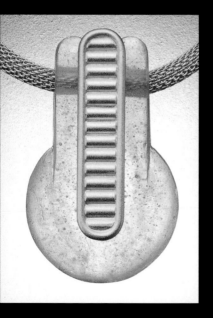

top
Mesh Necklace, 1997
acid polished transparent marine
blue pâte de verre glass,
24k gold plated brass
pendant 4 inches
Collection Kathy Gutow

bottom
Mesh Necklace, 1997
acid polished transparent light
green pâte de verre glass,
24k gold plated brass
pendant 4 inches
Collection of the Artist

Linda Schlanger

Mesh Necklace, 1995
acid polished gray & yellow glass,
24k gold plated brass
pendant 3 inches
with earrings
Collection Linda & Dr. Richard Schlanger

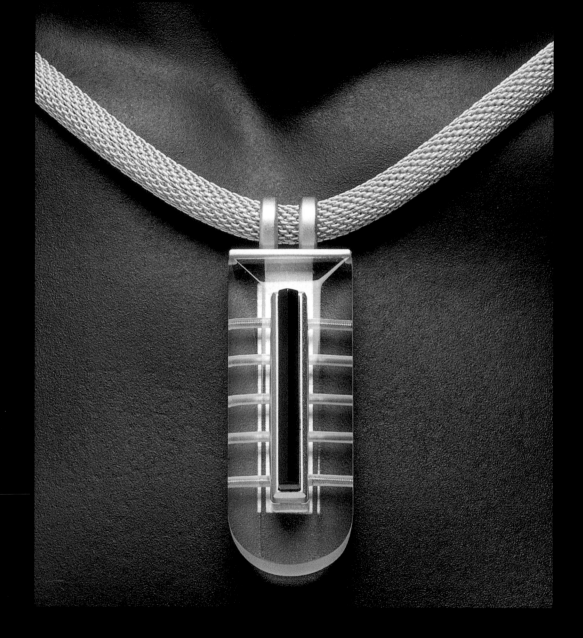

Mesh Necklace, 1995
polished clear & red glass,
24k gold plated brass
pendant 3 inches
with earrings
Collection Julie Lewis, M.D.

Cindy Riley

Mesh Necklace, 1995
acid polished clear glass, polished clear
mirrored glass detail, 24k gold plated brass
pendant 2 inches
with earrings
Collection Cindy & Dr. Tom Riley

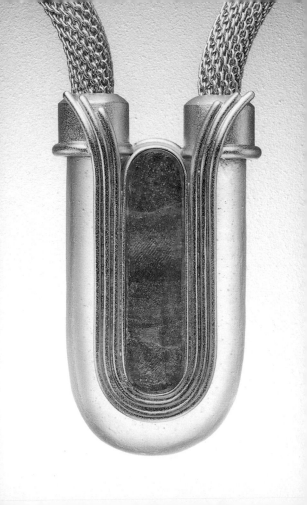

Gail M. Viditz-Ward

opposite
Mesh Necklace, 1997
acid polished lavender glass, clear pâte de verre glass,
24k gold plated brass
pendant 4 inches
with earrings
Collection Gail & Bud Viditz-Ward

Mesh Necklace, 1995
acid polished clear & lavender glass,
24k gold plated brass
pendant 3 inches

Dr. Arlene Silvers

Mesh Necklace, 1995
acid polished clear glass, polished transparent pink
optical glass, polished clear mirrored glass detail,
24k gold plated brass
pendant 2 inches
with earrings
Collection Drs. Arlene & Norman Silvers

Mesh Necklace, 1995
acid polished clear glass, polished forest
green glass, polished onyx detail,
24k gold plated brass
pendant 3 inches
Collection Doris Rief

Mesh Necklace, 1995
acid polished clear optical glass,
polished red glass, onyx detail,
24k gold plated brass
pendant 2 inches
with earrings
Collection Simona & Jerry Chazen

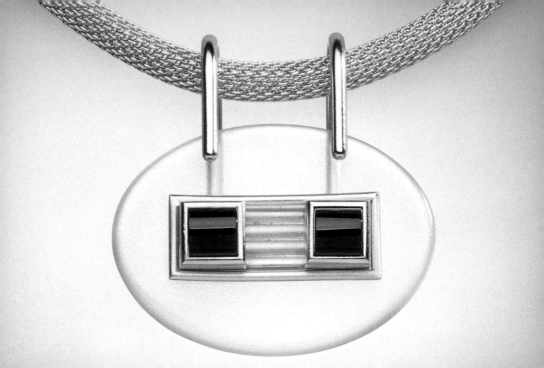

Joan Gordon

opposite
Mesh Necklace, 1997
acid polished clear glass, polished black
Vitrolite glass, 24k gold plated brass
pendant 3 inches
with earrings
Collection Joan & Donald Gordon

Pat Hubbard

Mesh Necklace, 1995
acid polished yellow & green pâte
de verre glass, 24k gold plated brass
pendant 2 inches
with earrings
Collection Pat Hubbard

Susan Sanders, Esq.

Mesh Necklace, 1996
acid polished transparent pink glass, polished clear
glass detail, 24k gold plated brass
pendant 3 inches
with earrings
Collection Susan & Fred Sanders

top
Mesh Necklace, 1996
acid polished clear glass, polished
glass detail, 24k gold plated brass
pendant 3 inches
with earrings
Collection Beverly & Sam Ross

bottom
Mesh Necklace, 1996
acid polished clear glass, polished
laminated clear & blue glass,
red paint detail, 24k gold plated brass
pendant 3 inches
Collection Jane & George Russell

Olivia Fischer

Mesh Necklace
Acid polished clear glass;
polished pink & clear mirrored glass detail,
24k gold plated brass
pendant: 3 inches
with earrings
1996
Collection of Olivia & Harlan Fischer

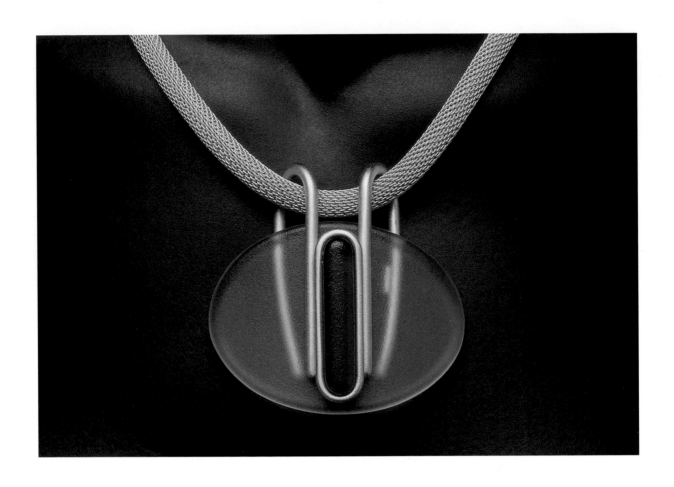

Mesh Necklace, 1996
acid polished clear & purple glass,
24k gold plated brass
pendant 3 inches
with earrings
Collection Ann & Robert Friedman,
promised to Cleveland Museum of Art

Jean Sosin

Mesh Necklace, 1997
acid polished clear optical glass,
polished black Vitrolite glass detail,
24k gold plated brass
pendant 3 inches
with earrings
Collection Jean Sosin

top
Mesh Necklace, 1995
polished opaque black glass,
polished pink mirrored glass detail,
24k gold plated brass
pendant 2 inches
Private Collection

Lea Minzter

Mesh Necklace, 1996
acid polished clear glass, polished clear
mirrored glass detail, 24k gold plated brass
pendant 3 inches
Collection Leatrice & Albert Minzter

Rhoda Epstein

Mesh Necklace, 1997
polished opaque light purple/black Vitrolite glass,
24k gold plated brass
pendant 3 inches
with earrings
Collection Rhoda & Stan Epstein

Joan Baxt

Mesh Necklace, 1996
polished opaque red/black Vitrolite glass,
polished clear mirrored glass detail,
24k gold plated brass
pendant 3 inches
Collection Joan & Milton Baxt

Myrna R. Leven

Mesh Necklace, 1996
acid polished clear glass, polished clear
mirrored glass detail, 24k gold plated brass
pendant 3 inches
Collection Myrna & David Leven

Dr. Susan Krevoy

opposite
Mesh Necklace, 1997
polished opaque black/purple Vitrolite glass,
24k gold plated brass
pendant 3 inches
Collection Dr. Susan Krevoy & Leo Spiwak

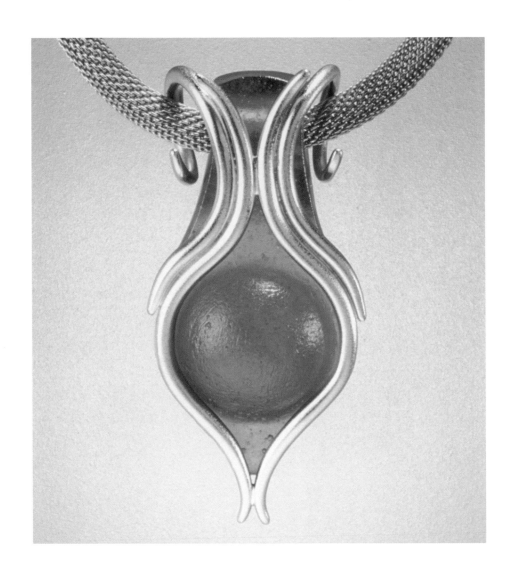

Mesh Necklace, 2000
acid polished green pâte de verre glass,
24k gold plated brass
pendant 3 inches
Collection Barbara & Alan Boroff

Mesh Necklace, 2000
acid polished purple & brown pâte de verre glass,
polished black Vitrolite glass, 24k gold plated brass
pendant 3 inches
with earrings

Mesh Necklace, 1998
acid polished clear glass, acid polished green
pâte de verre glass, 24k gold plated brass
pendant 3 inches
Collection Deborra & Marc Howard

Patricia Harris

Mesh Necklace, 1998
acid polished clear glass, acid polished green
pâte de verre glass, 24k gold plated brass
pendant 3 inches
with earrings
Collection Patricia Harris

Kathy Sackheim

Mesh Necklace, 1998
acid polished clear glass, acid polished green
pâte de verre glass, 24k gold plated brass
pendant 3 inches
Collection Kathy Sackheim

Pam Johnson

Mesh Necklace, 1995
polished transparent ruby red & cobalt blue glass,
24k gold plated brass
7 inches diam.
pendant 2 inches
with earrings
Collection Pam & William Johnson

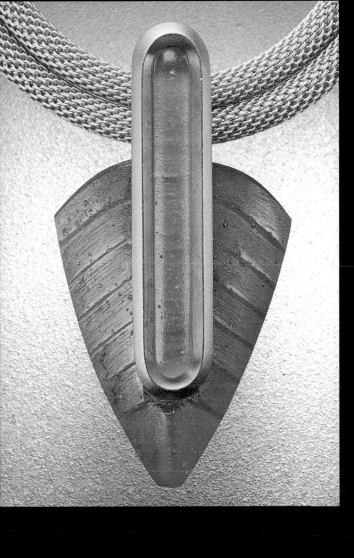

Mesh Necklace, 1998
acid polished gray/blue glass & lavender pâte de verre
glass, 24k gold plated brass
pendant 3 inches
Collection Pam & William Johnson

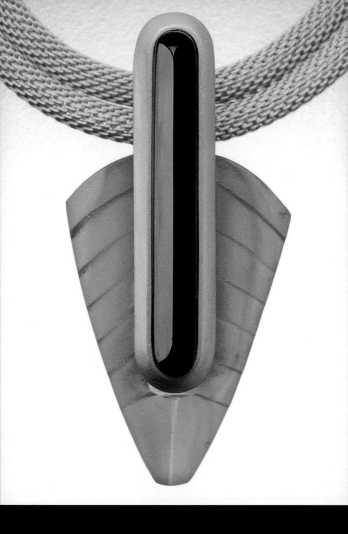

Mesh Necklace, 1997
acid polished amber pâte de verre glass,
polished black Vitrolite glass detail,
24k gold plated brass
pendant 3 inches
Collection of the Artist

Gail Silverman

Mesh Necklace, 1997
acid polished clear pâte de verre glass, acid
polished lavender pâte de verre glass detail,
24k gold plated brass
pendant 3 inches
with earrings
Collection Gail Silverman

Mesh Necklace, 1996
Acid polished lavender pâte de verre glass,
polished blue glass, 24k gold plated brass
pendant 2 inches
Collection Toledo Museum of Art,
donated by Maxine & William Block

Mesh Necklace, 2001
Acid polished amber & purple pâte de verre glass,
24k gold plated brass
pendant 3 inches
Collection Ruth Conant

Bright Beginning Floral Necklace, 2001
acid polished light green & clear pâte de verre glass,
24k gold plated brass
6 1/2 inches diam.
pendant 3 inches

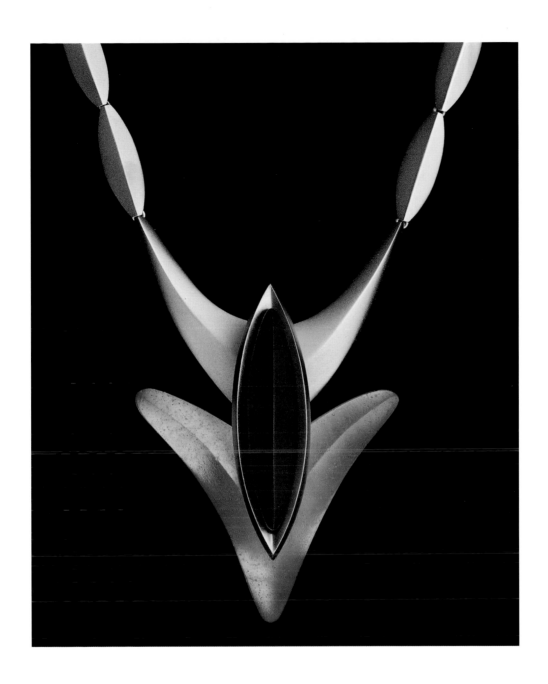

Tropical Flower Floral Necklace, 2001
acid polished aqua & red pâte de verre glass,
24k gold plated brass
6 1/2 inches diam.
pendant 3 inches
Collection Jacqueline & Robert Kaufman

Barbara Tober

opposite
Mesh Necklace, 2001
acid polished clear glass, polished black Vitrolite glass,
onyx details, 24k gold plated brass
pendant 3 inches
with earrings
Collection Heather Kaye Jacobs & Alan Jacobs

Mesh Necklace, 2000
acid polished clear glass, acid polished
purple pâte de verre glass, onyx details,
24k gold plated brass, 14k gold details
pendant 3 inches
with earrings
Collection Barbara & Donald Tober

Leisa Austin

opposite
Mesh Necklace, 2001
acid polished green pâte de verre glass,
polished black Vitrolite glass,
24k gold plated brass
pendant 3 inches
with earrings
Collection Leisa Austin

Karen Jenkins-Johnson

opposite
Mesh Necklace, 2001
acid polished clear & lavender glass, onyx detail,
24k gold plated brass
pendant 3 inches
with earrings
Collection Karen Jenkins-Johnson & Kevin D. Johnson

Linda J. Boone

opposite
Good Fortune Floral Necklace, 2000
acid polished transparent green glass,
clear pâte de verre glass; onyx details,
24k gold plated brass
6 inches diam., pendant 3 inches
with earrings
Collection Linda J. Boone

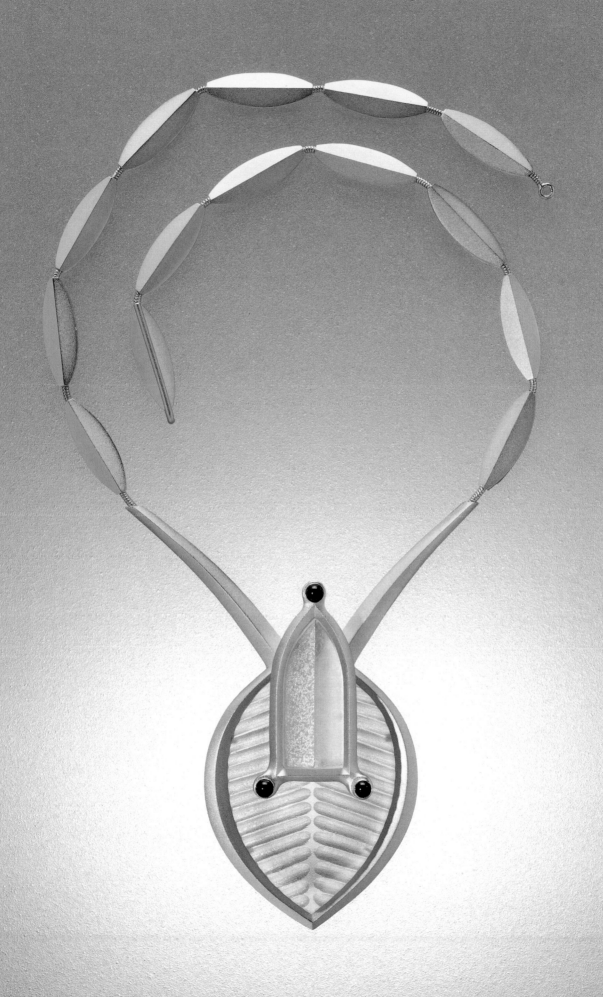

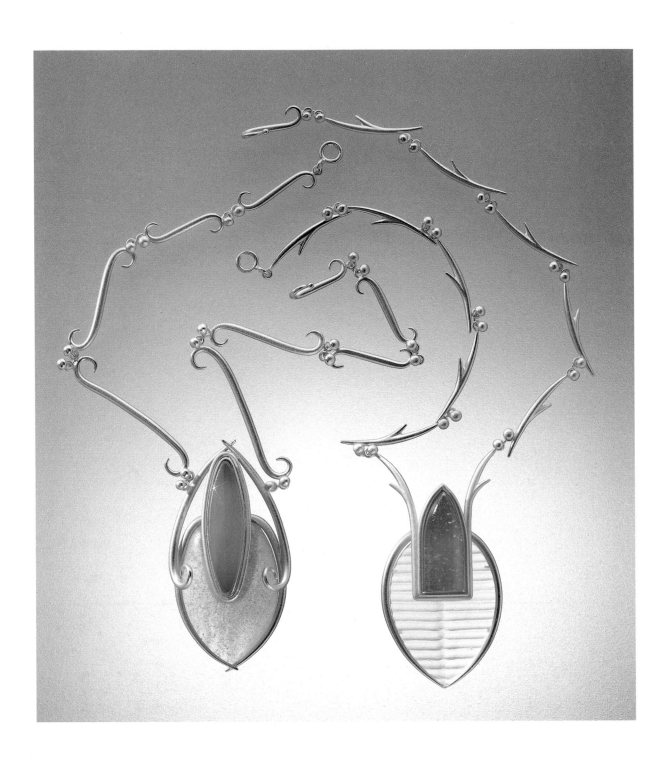

left
Iris Temple Floral Necklace, 2000
acid polished lavender pâte de verre
& clear glass, 24k gold plated brass
6 inches diam., pendant 3 inches
with earrings
Collection Dina & William Weisberger

right
Chelsea Floral Necklace, 2000
acid polished transparent clear glass,
acid polished peach pâte de verre glass,
24k gold plated brass
6 inches diam., pendant 3 inches

Calla Lily Floral Necklace, 2000
acid polished clear & transparent pink glass,
24k gold plated brass
pendant/brooch 3 inches
Collection Linda & Henry Wasserstein

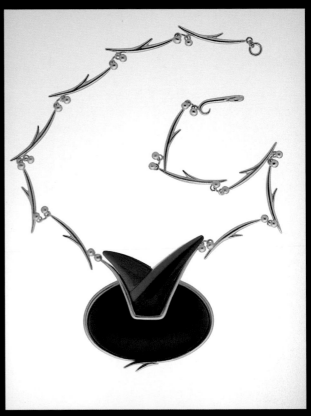

top
Primary Blossom Floral Necklace, 2001
acid polished transparent red, blue,
yellow, black Vitrolite glass,
24k gold plated brass

bottom
Cactus Flower Floral Necklace, 2001
polished laminated orange, red, green,
blue, purple Vitrolite glass, acid polished
black Vitrolite glass, 24k gold plated brass

opposite
Nile Bud Floral Necklace, 2001
acid polished clear, blue, & orange
transparent glass, 24k gold plated brass
6 inches diam., pendant/brooch 3 inches

Mimi West

opposite
Water Leaf Floral Necklace, 2000
acid polished black opaque Vitrolite glass,
transparent green-yellow pâte de verre glass,
24k gold plated brass
pendant/brooch 3 inches
with earrings
Collection Pam & William Johnson

Pink Amazonia Floral Necklace, 2000
acid polished black opaque Vitrolite glass,
acid polished transparent neodymium glass,
24k gold plated brass
pendant/brooch 3 inches
with earrings
Collection Mimi & Bernie West

Libby Cooper

opposite
Crown Imperial Floral Necklace, 2000
polished black & multicolored
Vitrolite glass, 24k gold plated brass
6 inches diam., pendant 3 inches
Collection Libby Cooper

JoAnne Cooper

Geometric Carnival Nexus Necklace, 1999
acid polished multicolored transparent glass,
polished opaque black Vitrolite glass,
24k gold plated brass
7 inches diam.
with earrings
Collection JoAnne Cooper

Half Moon Brooch, 2001
acid polished clear glass, polished black
Vitrolite glass, 24k gold plated brass
pendant/brooch 2 inches
with earrings

Mesh Necklace, 2001
Polished black Vitrolite glass, polished green
pâte de verre glass, 24k gold plated brass
pendant 2 inches
with earrings
Collection Jean Garrus

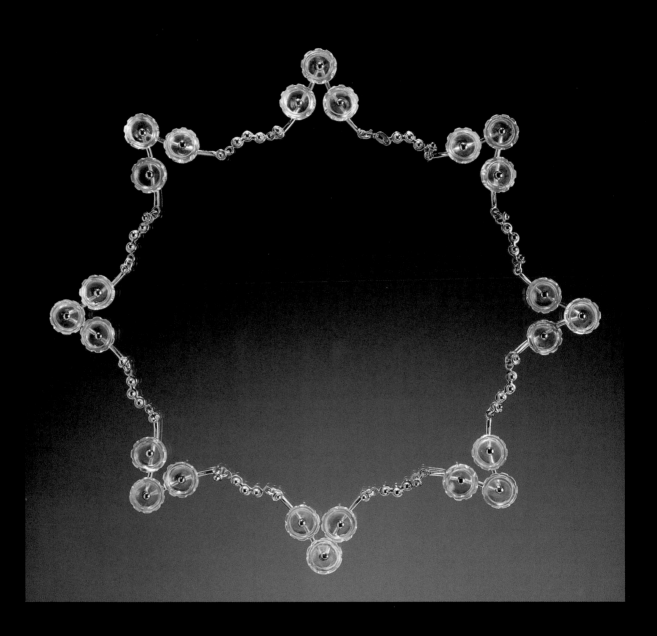

Snowflake Necklace, 1999
acid polished, clear Waterford Crystal,
18k yellow gold
6 1/2 inches diam.

Millie Andreu

Lotus Necklace, 1999
polished clear Waterford Crystal, polished
sterling silver
9 inches diam., pendant 2 1/2 inches
Collection Millie & Joseph Andreu

Lotus Necklace, 1999
polished clear Waterford Crystal, polished purple
glass detail, 14k yellow gold
7 inches diam.
Collection Cleveland Museum of Art,
donated by Waterford Crystal Ltd., and Linda MacNeil
in honor of Ann Friedman

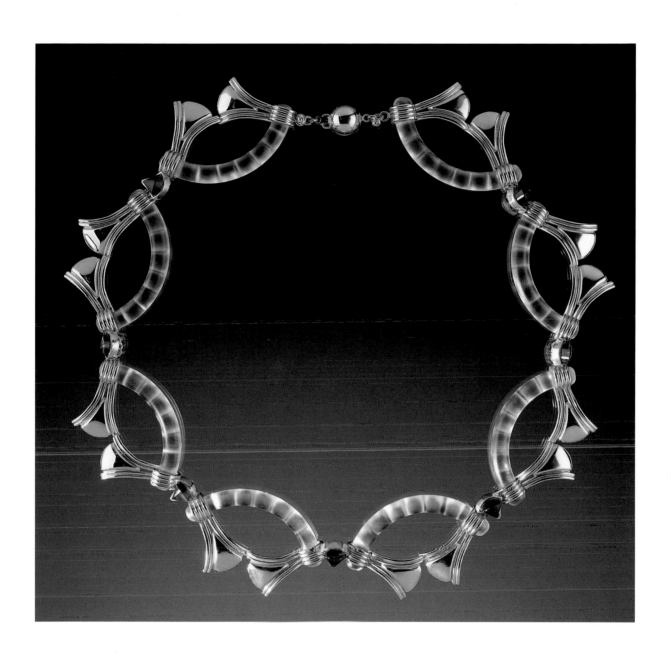

above & cover
Lotus Necklace, 1999
acid polished clear Waterford Crystal,
polished green glass detail, 14k yellow gold
6 1/2 inches diam.
Collection Mint Museum of Craft and Design,
donated by Waterford Crystal Ltd. & Linda MacNeil
in honor of Chris Rifkin

Vera Loeffler

opposite
Lotus Brooch, 1999
polished clear Waterford Crystal, 18k yellow gold
3 x 2 inches
with earrings
Collection Vera & Dr. Robert Loeffler

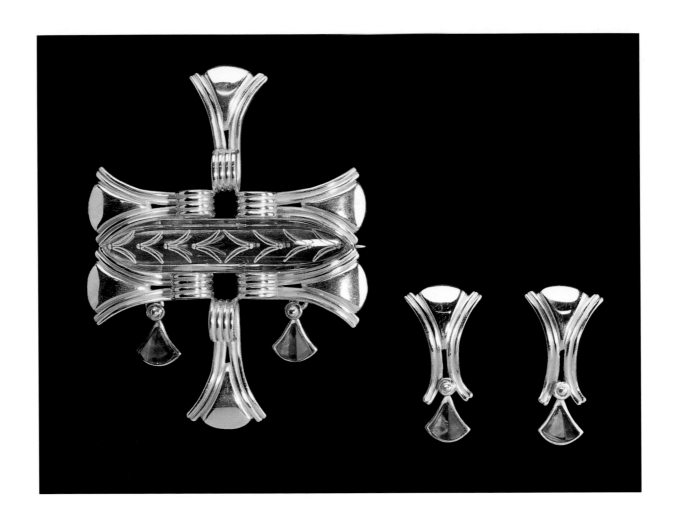

Lotus of Alexander Brooch, 2002
polished tinted lavendar optical glass,
polished 18k yellow gold
3 x 2 x 1/2 inches
with earrings

opposite
Blue Nile Brooch, 2002
polished clear & blue optical glass,
polished 18k yellow gold
4 x 1 1/4 x 1/2 inches
with earrings
Collection Carolyn J. & Robert Springborn

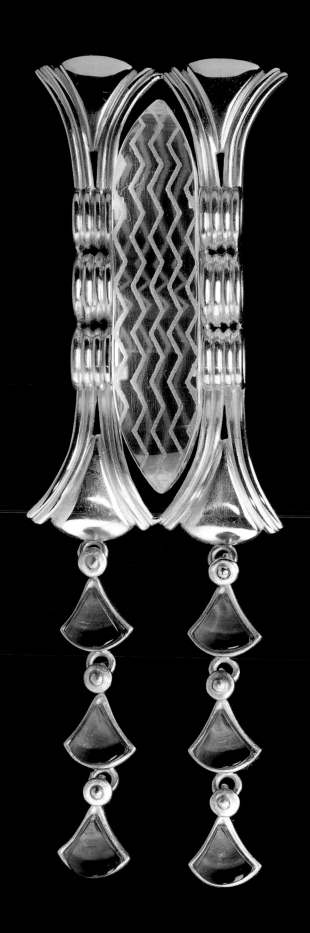

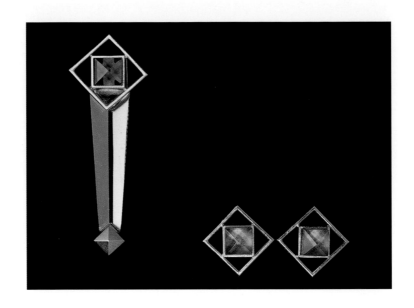

top
Fibula Blue Brooch, 2001
polished clear & blue transparent glass,
24k gold plated brass
4 inches
with earrings

bottom
Victorian Oval Brooch, 2001
acid polished yellow tinted glass,
polished green transparent glass,
24k gold plated brass
2 1/2 inches
with earrings

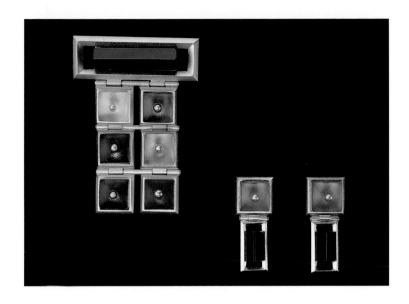

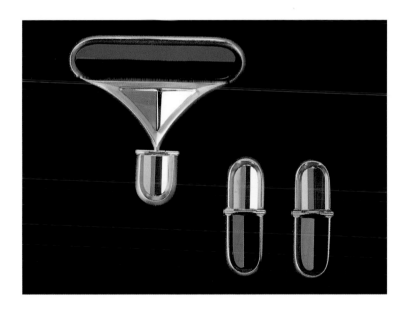

top
Puzzle Brooch, 2001
acid polished multicolored transparent
glass, polished black Vitrolite glass,
24k gold plated brass
2 1/4 x 1 1/2 inches
with earrings

bottom
Pink Drops Brooch, 2001
polished pink mirrored glass,
polished black Vitrolite glass,
24k gold plated brass
2 1/2 x 2 1/2 inches
with earrings

inda MacNeil studied at the Philadelphia College of Art, now The University of the Arts, the Massachusetts College of Art, and received her B.F.A. at the Rhode Island School of Design in 1976. Her work has been featured in *American Craft, Craft Horizons,* and major articles have appeared in *Neues Glas, Metalsmith* and numerous other magazines and publications. MacNeil's accomplishments have been recognized by both the Massachusetts Council on the Arts and the National Endowment for the Arts. She has exhibited extensively in respected galleries nationwide and has taught and lectured throughout the United States and Japan. Her works are in numerous museum collections including the American Craft Museum, New York; Victoria and Albert Museum, London; the Metropolitan Museum of Art, New York; and the Museum of Fine Arts, Boston.

Solo Exhibitions

2001	Riley Hawk Galleries, Columbus, OH
	South Shore Art Center, Cohasset, MA (Dailey/MacNeil Archival Selections)
	Habatat Galleries, Boca Raton, FL
2000	Paul Mellon Arts Center Gallery, Choate Rosemary Hall, Wallingford, CT
	(Dailey/MacNeil Archival Selections)
1999	The Art Center in Hargate, St. Paul's School, Concord, NH
	(Dailey/MacNeil Archival Selections)
1998	Riley Hawk Galleries, Columbus, OH
	Leo Kaplan Modern, New York, NY
1997	Habatat Galleries, Boca Raton, FL
1996	Imago Gallery, Palm Desert, CA
	Riley Hawk Galleries, Cleveland, OH
1995	Habatat Galleries, Boca Raton, FL
	Vespermann Gallery, Atlanta, GA
	Imago Gallery, Palm Desert, CA
1993	Riley Hawk Galleries, Cleveland, OH
1988	Helen Drutt Gallery, Philadelphia, PA
1986	Anne O'Brien Gallery, Washington, DC
1985	Heller Gallery, New York, NY
1984	Habatat Galleries, Bay Harbor, FL
1983	David Bernstein Gallery, Boston, MA
	Kurland/Summers Gallery, Los Angeles, CA
1981	Habatat Galleries, Lathrup Village, MI
1980	Julie: Artisan's Gallery, New York, NY
1979	Ten Arrow Gallery, Cambridge, MA

Selected Group Exhibitions

2003-04	"The Art of Gold"
	January-May 2003, Crocker Art Museum, Sacramento, CA
	September-October 2003, University of Richmond Museums, Richmond, VA
	January-March 2004, The Arkansas Arts Center, Little Rock, AR
2001	"SOFA," Chicago, New York City, Leo Kaplan Modern, NYC
	"The 19th Annual International Glass Invitational," Habatat Galleries, Boca Raton, FL
	"Hot Glass," Mobilia Gallery, Cambridge, MA
2000	"SOFA," Chicago, New York City, Leo Kaplan Modern, NYC
	"Structure, Symbol & Substance," Mobilia Gallery, Cambridge, MA
	"Millennium Glass: An International Survey of Studio Glass," Kentucky Art and
	Craft Foundation, Louisville, KY (traveling exhibition)
	"The 18th Annual International Glass Invitational," Habatat Galleries, Boca Raton, FL

1999	"50 Years of Studio Jewelry," Mobilia Gallery, Cambridge, MA
	"SOFA," Chicago, Leo Kaplan Modern, NYC
	"Glass! Glorious Glass!," Renwick Gallery, Washington, DC
	"New Perspectives/Ancient Medium," Tampa, FL
	"Sculptural Bias," Grand Central Gallery, Tampa, FL
	Grand Opening - selected artist, Riley Hawk Gallery, Kirkland, WA
1998	"SOFA," Chicago, Leo Kaplan Modern, NYC
	"15th International Glass Invitational," Habatat Galleries, Boca Raton, FL
1997	"Celebrating American Craft 1975-1995," American Craft Museum, NYC
1996	"An Historic View," Mobilia Gallery, Cambridge, MA
	"Glass: The Cutting Edge," Clark Gallery, Lincoln, MA
	"SOFA," Chicago, Leo Kaplan Modern, NYC
	"SOFA," Miami, Leo Kaplan Modern, NYC
	"Glass: New England," Worcester Center for Crafts, MA
	"Sculptural Forms in Glass," Joanne Rapp Gallery, Scottsdale, AZ
1995	"SOFA," Miami, Miller Gallery, Creative Glass Center of America, Millville, NJ
	"Jewelry," Mobilia Gallery, Cambridge, MA
	"SOFA," Chicago, Leo Kaplan Modern, NYC
1994	"Jewelry," Miller Gallery, NYC
	"Spring Opening," Hanover Gallery, Hanover, NH
	"One-of-a-Kind Jewelry," Mobilia Gallery, Cambridge, MA
	"Jewelry," Leo Kaplan Modern, NYC
	"SOFA," Chicago, Miller Gallery, NYC
	"SOFA," Chicago, Leo Kaplan Modern, NYC
1993	"Jewelry," Riley Hawk Galleries, Cleveland, OH
	"New Art Forms," Chicago, Leo Kaplan Modern, NYC
	"The Jewelry Project," Creative Glass Center of America, Millville, NJ
	"Precious Art to Wear," Habatat Shaw Gallery, Pontiac, MI
	"Sculptural/Functional Show," Helander Gallery, Palm Beach, FL
1992	"Wearables," American Craft Museum, NYC
1991	"Jewelry," Wheeler-Seidel Gallery, NYC
1990	"Tables & Jewelry," Gallery of Function Art, Santa Monica, CA
	"Holiday Show," Vespermann Gallery, Atlanta, GA
	"Inaugural Exhibition," Leo Kaplan Modern, NYC
1988	"The Sixteenth Annual International Glass Invitational," Habatat Galleries, Lathrup Village, MI
1986	"Poetry of the Physical," American Craft Museum, NYC
	"Contemporary Crafts: A Concept in Flux," Pittsburgh, PA
	"Glass as Sculpture," Contemporary Crafts Assoc., Portland, OR
	"4th Annual National Invitational," Habatat Galleries, MI
	"Glass Exhibition," Eve Mannes Gallery, Atlanta, GA
1985	"Glass Now '85" Hokkaido Museum of Modern Art, Sapporo, Japan
	"Architecture of the Vessel," Rochester Institute of Technology, Rochester, NY
	"Art du Verre," Musee Des Beaux Arts, Rouen, France
	"International Glass Jewelry," Coleridge of Highgate, London, England
	"MacNeil, Harper, Rustadler," David Bernstein Gallery, Boston, MA
	"3rd Annual Invitational National," Habatat Galleries, MI
	"National Invitational," Elaine Potter Gallery, San Francisco, CA
	"Worked With Gold 2," Quadrum Gallery, Chestnut Hill, MA

1984	"Jewelry USA," American Craft Museum, NYC touring USA and Asia
	"Sculptural Glass," Elaine Potter Gallery, San Francisco, CA
1983	"American Glass," United States Embassy, Prague, Czechoslovakia
	"5th Annual National Exhibition," Contemporary Artisans Gallery, San Francisco, CA
	"Glass National," Habatat Galleries, Lathrup Village, MI
1982	"International Directions in Glass Art," Gallery of Western Australia, Perth, Australia
	"Pilchuck Glass," Traver Sutton Gallery, Seattle, WA
	"Contemporary American Glass," Young Gallery, San Jose, CA
	"Masters in Glass," Human Arts Gallery, Dallas, TX
	"Glass National," Habatat Galleries, Pontiac, MI
	"4th Annual National Exhibition," Contemporary Artisans Gallery, San Francisco, CA
1981	"American Art at its Best: Glass," American Art, Inc., Atlanta, GA
	"National Invitational," Ivor Kurland Gallery, Los Angeles, CA
	"7 From Glass Routes," Clark Gallery, Lincoln, MA
	"Americans in Glass," Leigh Yawkey Woodson Art Museum, Wausau, WI
	"Glass Routes," DeCordova Museum, Lincoln, MA
	"Good as Gold," Renwick Gallery, Washington, DC
	"Women Working in Glass," Contemporary Artisans Gallery, San Francisco, CA
	"Glass National," Habatat Galleries, Pontiac, MI
	"3rd Annual National Exhibition," Contemporary Artisans Gallery, San Francisco, CA
1980	"Art for Use," Lake Placid Olympics, NY
	"Fragile Art," First Prize: Mixed Media, Portcon, San Francisco, CA
	"New American Glass: Focus Glass Art Society," Huntington, WV
	"Art as Body Adornment," University of Delaware, Newark, DE

Awards

2001	Excellence in Jewelry Metalwork, The University of the Arts, Philadelphia, PA
2001	Art of Liberty Award, National Liberty Museum, Philadelphia, PA
1985	National Endowment for the Arts Fellowship
1981	Massachusetts Council on the Arts Fellowship

Selected Articles, Reviews, and Publications

2001	Gorfinkle, Constance, "Double Vision," The Patriot Ledger, May 12-13, Weekend Entertainment, pp.47-48
	Jacobson, Seth, "Glass with Class," Hingham Journal, May 10, p. 23
	"The Heart and Art of Glass," Beverly Hills Forum Series, April 23
	Liu, Robert K. and Minson, James, "Contemporary Glass Jewelry, A Continuing Tradition," Ornament, Volume 24, No. 3, Spring; pp. 40-45
2000	Eddins, Liz, "Marriage of the Minds," Views, RISD, Fall; pp. 14-15
	Rausa Fuller, Janet, "Cutting-edge Jewelry Captures the Art," Chicago Sun-Times, Nov. 2, pp. 42-43

1999	Whitney, D. Quincy, "Shapes of Fantasy Emerge from Glass," The Boston Sunday Globe, Jan. 17, pNH14
	"Dan Dailey and Linda MacNeil: Art in Glass and Metal," Printed on the occasion of the exhibition at The Art Center at Hargate, St. Paul's School. A catalog showcasing the artist's works and processes.
	MacDonald, Sarah, "A Delightful Duo," The Pelican, Vol. XLXV
	O'Sullivan, Michael, "Masters of Accessible Arts," Washington Post Weekend, October 22, "On Exhibit," Renwick Gallery, Washington, DC
1996	Chambers, Karen, "A Detailed Look," Metalsmith, Spring; pp. 24-33
1994	Lewis, Susan Grant, "One of a Kind: American Art Jewelry Today," p. 19
1993	"A Matter of Scale: Innovations in American Glass Jewelry," Glass Work, No. 15, pp. 18-25
1989	Klien, Dan, "Glass, A Contemporary Art," pp. 44, 71
	Frantz, Susanne K., "Contemporary Glass," p. 94
	Kuroki, Rika, "Linda MacNeil," Glass Work, October; pp. 17-21
	American Craft Council/Museum, "Craft Today USA," p. 126
1988	Mayer, Barbara, "Contemporary American Craft Art," pp. 25, 27
1986	Stern, Robert A. M., "International Design Yearbook," p.130-131
	Bizot, Chantal, "Bijoux de verre, un tour d'horizon," Ceramique et Du Verre, May/June; pp. 16-22
	Lucie-Smith, Edward; Smith, Paul J., "Craft Today; Poetry of the Physical," American Craft Museum
1985	Lonier, Terri, "Artistic Innovation in Glass," Neues Glas, February; pp. 60-66
1984	Lonier, Terri, "Jewelry as Wearable Art," Robb Report, August; pp. 49-54
	Hampson, Ferdinand, "Glass: State of the Art," p. 63
1983	Woell, J. Fred, "Linda MacNeil: New Work," Metalsmith, Fall; p. 47
	Yoshimizu, Tsuneo, "Linda MacNeil's Glass Works," Four Seasons of Jewelry; No. 48
	Bernstein, Ruby, "Sculptural Glass," American Art Glass Quarterly, Fall; p. 68

Guest Lectures

2002	Carnegie Museum of Art, Pittsburgh, PA
2001	The University of the Arts, Philadelphia, PA
	South Shore Arts Center, Cohasset, MA
	Beverly Hills Forum Series, Beverly Hills Hotel, Beverly Hills, CA
2000	New York Times Inside Culture Club, New York, NY
	Paul Mellon Arts Center Gallery, Choate Rosemary Hall, Wallingford, CT
1999	Waterford Crystal, Waterford, Ireland
1998	St. Paul's School, Concord, NH
	Tyler School of Art, Elkins Park, PA
1989	Faculty, Pilchuck Glass School, Stanwood, WA
	Miasa Center, Miasa, Japan
	Niijima Glass Center, Niijima, Japan

1986	Rhode Island School of Design, RI
	Haystack Mountain School of Crafts, Deer Isle, ME
1985	British Glass Society, England
1984	Massachusetts College of Art, Boston, MA
1983	Philadelphia College of Art, Philadelphia, PA
1979-82	Program in Artisanry, Boston University, Boston, MA
1978-82	Pilchuck School, Seattle, WA

Collections

American Craft Museum, New York, NY
Corning Museum of Glass, Corning, NY
Detroit Institute of Art, Detroit, MI
Les Archives de la Cristallerie Daum, Nancy and Paris, France
Mint Museum of Craft and Design, Charlotte, NC
Museum of Fine Arts, Boston, MA
Renwick Gallery, National Museum of Art, Smithsonian Institute, Washington, D.C.
J. B. Speed Art Museum, Louisville, KY
The Cleveland Museum of Art, Cleveland, OH
The Metropolitan Museum of Art, New York, NY
Toledo Museum of Art, Toledo, OH
Victoria and Albert Museum, London, England
Waterford Crystal, Waterford, Ireland
Racine Museum of Arts, Racine, WI
Numerous private collections

Gallery Representation

Habatat Galleries, Boca Raton, FL and Great Barrington, MA
Imago Galleries, Palm Desert, CA
Leo Kaplan Modern, New York, NY
Hawk Gallery, Columbus, OH
Mobilia Gallery, Cambridge, MA

Sponsors

Leisa Austin
Imago Galleries

Lois Boardman
Boardman Family

Linda J. Boone
Habatat Galleries, Florida

Joanne Cooper
Mobilia Gallery

Libby Cooper
Mobilia Gallery

Susan Crowell

Daphne Farago
Farago Foundation

MeraLee Goldman

Scott Jacobson
Leo Kaplan Modern

Karen Jenkins-Johnson
Jenkins Johnson Gallery

Pam Johnson

Susan Krevoy

Mimi S. Livingston

Anna Mendel

Chris Rifkin

Arlene and Norman Silvers

Jean Sosin

Carolyn J. Springborn

Delores Stiles

Mimi West

Acknowledgments

Susan and Fred Sanders
Counsel

Mark Lyman and Anne Meszko
Expressions of Culture Inc.

Suzane Ramljak
Author

Helen W. Drutt English
Forword

Joe Rapone
Art Director, Book Design

John Carlano
Portrait Photography

Angella Mendillo
Portrait Make-up

Susie Cushner
Studio Photography

Charles Mayer
Studio Photography

Bill Truslow
Studio Photography

Scott Jacobson
Leo Kaplan Modern Gallery

Linda J. Boone
Habatat Galleries

Leisa and David Austin
Imago Galleries

Natalie and Dr. Warren Werbitt

Chris Chandler
Studio Glass Assistant

Pam Blake
Studio Office Assistant

The Honorable MeraLee Goldman, Mayor
Henry Korn, Director of Art and Culture
City of Beverly Hills Cultural Center

Index of Portraits

Index of Works

back cover
Mirrored Glass Necklace, 1995
polished clear mirrored glass, 14k yellow gold
7 inches diam.
with earrings
Collection of the Artist